JM STELLAR

ONE WOMAN'S JOURNEY TO
THE TRUTH ABOUT HOMOSEXUALITY

WHEN I SAID *Yes* TO THE HOLY SPIRIT

Published by Innovo Publishing, LLC
www.innovopublishing.com
1-888-546-2111

Providing Full-Service Publishing Services for
Christian Authors, Artists & Ministries: Books, eBooks, Audiobooks, Music & Film

WHEN I SAID YES TO THE HOLY SPIRIT:
One Woman's Journey to the Truth About Homosexuality

Copyright © 2017 by JM Stellar
All rights reserved.

No part of this publication may be reproduced, stored in a retrieval system, or transmitted in any form or by any means electronic, mechanical, photocopying, recording, or otherwise, without the prior written permission of the author.

Scripture taken from the NEW AMERICAN STANDARD BIBLE®, Copyright © 1960,1962,1963,1968,1971,1972,1973,1975,1977,1995 by The Lockman Foundation. Used by permission.

ISBN: 978-1-61314-406-0

Cover Design & Interior Layout: Innovo Publishing, LLC

Printed in the United States of America
U.S. Printing History
First Edition: November 2017

*"I plead with you—never,
ever give up on hope,
never doubt, never tire,
and never become discouraged.
Be not afraid."*

—*St. John Paul II*

"Therefore if anyone is in Christ, he is a new creature; the old things passed away; behold, new things have come."

—*2 Corinthians 5:17*

Contents

Acknowledgements 7

Prologue 9

1. Seeds Planted and Watered 13
2. Potential Tree of Evil Nurtured and Manifested 19
3. Branching Out 23
4. The Discovery and Absorption of the Light 35
5. Gradually Growing Into Good 43
6. Withstanding the Storms 63
7. Blows Along My Bark 73
8. Basking in the Warmth of God's Rays 83

Author's Afterword 89

References 101

Organization References 103

Christian Ministry References 105

Other Organizations 107

Acknowledgements

    I would like to thank my sister Lonnie, who God used as a messenger to call me to follow Him. She has been my constant source of support and encouragement during the early stages of my healing process, and she always reassured me that I was "in God's grace." She has also been my source of accountability throughout, without whom I would have most definitely given up.

    I would also like to thank my sister Marissa and my mother Maribel for always being there for me, for never hesitating to lend an ear, for not letting me lose hope.

    Most of all, I would like to thank almighty God, for saving me from living the life of a lie, from a lifestyle that is abominable to Him, and for revealing the Truth to me.

> *Call to me and I will answer you, and I will tell you great and mighty things, which you do not know. (Jeremiah 33:3)*

Prologue

I wrote this book to offer hope and encouragement that there *is* freedom from homosexuality through a relationship with Jesus Christ. I want to share that there *is* a way out if you decide not to live that way. This message is about the transforming power of Jesus Christ.

Recently I learned that only about 33 percent of the US population has experienced a true transformation from God in their lives. In this day and age, with the legalization of homosexual marriage in most states and the transgenderism becoming more and more relevant and accepted, this information is needed more than ever. We are all born at a specific time and place on earth for a specific purpose from God. We are all called to be a light in a dark world. "You are the light of the world. A town built on a hill cannot be hidden. Neither do people light a lamp and put it under a bowl. Instead they put it on its stand, and it gives light to everyone in the house" (Matthew 5:14-15). We are also Christ's ambassadors. "Therefore, we are ambassadors for Christ, God making his appeal through us" (2 Corinthians 5:20). I believe it is my destiny now, at this moment in history, through the Holy Spirit, to shed this light upon you and to share with you the truth that He revealed to me.

You have a choice. "Then choose for yourselves this day whom you will serve" (Joshua 24:15). Twenty-two years ago I made that choice; I made a commitment to Jesus Christ. With the help of the Holy Spirit working through my oldest sister, Lonnie, I chose to follow Jesus' way—to give Him a chance. I did not want to live a homosexual lifestyle. I knew it would be hard, and

I knew it was going to be stressful, but I wanted to be "normal" like everyone else. Most of all, I knew down deep it was wrong.

I want to tell my life story as a testimony to those who need it and to be a witness to how God, through His grace, can change you. I compare the chapters of this book to the development of a tree, from the planting of the seeds to the maturation or fruit-producing stages. Immediately I get to the roots of the issue so you can understand and see similarities in your own life (or in the lives of people you care about). I describe in detail the steps leading up to the day I said yes to the Holy Spirit and exactly how my transformation took place. I disclose exactly what helped me and what I did during the growth process. I provide examples of my victories, breakthroughs, and downfalls. I offer practical ways on how to recognize temptation and how to overcome it. I share specific tactics that helped me. In addition, I note that because of original sin, we may stumble along the way and face roadblocks, but that does not mean that we veer off course. We do not have to turn around and go back! With God's help, we will make it through to our destination. Finally, I discuss how it is a lifelong journey. I like what Randy Pausch stated in his book, *The Last Lecture*: "We cannot change the cards we are dealt, just how we play the hand." We may never achieve perfection, but we can live a life of excellence. God is always working on us!

I hope and pray that you choose God's path; that you or someone who loves you "stumbles upon" this book as Lonnie "stumbled upon" the book that propelled me in the right direction; that this book helps you tremendously and is a blessing to you. I want to save souls. I want to show people the truth. I believe this is my life's assignment. At the end of my life, when I enter into the gates of heaven, I can't wait to hear the God of all creation say to me, "Well done, good and faithful servant. You have been faithful over a little; I will set you over much. Enter into the joy of your master" (Matthew 25:21). And I hope you want Him to tell you that too.

> *That, in reference to your former manner of life, you lay aside the old self, which is being corrupted in accordance with the lusts of deceit, and that you be renewed in the spirit of your mind, and put on the new self, which in the likeness of God has been created in righteousness and holiness of the truth. (Ephesians 4:22-24)*

1.
Seeds Planted and Watered

I am the youngest of three girls from a traditional Italian family. My mother's pregnancy was unplanned; I was a "happy surprise." When I learned this a few years later, I perceived it as being unwanted, which contributed to first feelings of low self-esteem. My father, coming from an old-fashioned Italian background, wanted a boy. He hoped any one of his children was going to be a boy, but more so me, since I was going to be the last one—his last hope. In fact, at one time he sponsored an impoverished boy overseas through the mail whose name was John. He thought of this boy as the son he never had.

At exactly two weeks old, I contracted an illness that landed me in the hospital for a little under a week. This separation from my mother as an infant established a lack of constant physical contact and feelings of protection from her—the most important person in a (female) newborn's life. This was not a direct cause, but might have opened a door to, the development of homosexuality, making me more susceptible. I lacked the first stage of feminine bonding.

In my early years, I wanted masculine toys for Christmas, such as cars, racetracks, guns, and tough action figures like the Incredible Hulk doll. I never liked regular dolls or feminine things. I remember sitting by my living room table and staring at a picture of Lou Ferrigno as *The Incredible Hulk* in *US* magazine and my father asking my mother, "Why is she staring at that so much?" Little did we know that I was bonding with this popular male figure at the time. I wanted to be a mail carrier like my father when I grew up. I also dressed kind of boyish, preferring loose-fitting jeans, flannel shirts, and T-shirts. I hated dresses and long hair. Most would argue that these are some clues to justify why one is inherently homosexual; many do not know that these are the first signs of *defensive detachment*, a term given by Elizabeth Moberly in her book, *Homosexuality: A New Christian Ethic*. More on that later.

My first female crush was a blonde-haired girl in the fourth grade. She was pretty, smart, and on-the-ball, and in some classes, the teacher's pet. She possessed things I didn't see in myself (although I was smart in school too). I was the shy, quiet one. In eighth grade, my peers dubbed the nickname "MUTE" on the back of my senior shirt. My first TV crush was Cindy Williams on *Laverne & Shirley*, which was the first revelation of my unmet love need from my mother. When my mother would sleep with me, as she often did (I was attached to her), I used to pretend Cindy was there too, and my mother was the landlord. I have no idea how I came up with that.

Because of the serious condition I was in as a baby, my mother was very over-protective of me. She constantly worried about me, and I remember her telling my sisters to "watch that kid!" when I went out with them. We were very close. At school, she was always there at lunchtime and always there to pick me up. I can remember the kids chanting, "JM, your mother! JM, your mother!" I was embarrassed all the time. Of course, I always *did* want her there. Any time I complained of the simplest

1. Seeds Planted and Watered

ailment, my mother brought me to the doctor. Every child wants attention, but I got *too much* attention. I unconsciously perceived her over-protectiveness as a bad thing. For me, it was an emotional hurt or wound that stunted my psychological growth. As Elizabeth Moberly explained in her aforementioned book, I was "emotionally crippled." And, because of this unhealthy bond (unmet love need), I couldn't form normal, same-sex friendships.

My father, on the other hand, was emotionally distant. I didn't feel close to him at all. If I did not have a close relationship and proper communication with the first man in my life, how could I with other men? I never verbally called him "Dad." I only wrote it in greeting cards. His way of thinking was that his only job was providing for the family financially; the mother did all the rest. This was no fault of his own. He loved us in the only way he knew how. He didn't show any physical or emotional signs of affection because he never received any as a child. He didn't affirm my femininity. He did, however, often praise me when I did great on tests and got excellent grades on my report card. I felt accepted when he did this.

Notice I used the word, *felt*. It was my perception. He did accept me; he just had a hard time showing it. That's probably part of the reason why I am an over-achiever to this day and feel most valued and self-worthy when I accomplish all the things on my daily "to do" list. Sometimes I still feel as if the world is crashing in if something doesn't get done as planned.

As the domineering figure in the family, usually my father's way went, and he often yelled to communicate it. He said, as many Italians do, "I'm not yelling, I'm just talking loud!" To me, it was yelling. My mother often spoke condescendingly and negatively about him to me during my formative years, venting as if I was her friend instead of her daughter. We shared everything, but she did not know the damage she was causing. I remember almost every night when she heard him walking down the alley way when he came home from work, she would say, "Oh no!"

This was primarily because he used to drink after work, and we never knew in what condition he would come home. I've picked up that same pattern of behavior towards him and often find myself saying that phrase to this day.

In relation to my father, my mother was usually passive. Her opinion didn't count. My father didn't listen to her. She was sweet and soft-spoken, very accommodating, and easy to get along with. To put it in other words, she was a wimp. I learned that most men and women with same-sex attraction often see others of the same-sex as victims. They see them, consciously or unconsciously, as victims of abuse (of any sort) from the opposite sex. I noticed that they feel an underlying pity towards them or feel that they are always justified and have an innate propensity to nurture and care for them. I noticed this by the way my male cousin with SSA (same-sex attraction) was treating my father in the hospital, and I remember my mother being so impressed.

Because my mother was submissive, I saw her as a doormat. I perceived her as fearful and subservient to men. I had a fear of men, and sexual activity, and marriage. In fact, when my mother and I used to pass by a wedding ceremony at a church or hear limos honking "Here Comes the Bride," we would say, "Poor fools!" I didn't think it was a good thing to be a woman. I didn't bond or identify with my mother. I detached myself from her, the most important first female figure in a daughter's life—according to Elizabeth Moberly—thus detaching myself from femininity. And this introduces the term *defensive detachment*. In doing so, I modeled myself after my masculine father, as girls who grow up to be lesbians often do. That's why many gay women "look" like men; they choose male hairstyles and clothing because subconsciously, they detach themselves from femininity and mimic masculinity. The opposite is true for the men.

What further contributed to my gender confusion was my uncle who was also my godfather. He lived next door and called

1. Seeds Planted and Watered

me "Sonny." It must have been the way I dressed or perhaps my short hair. Or, he wished I was a boy as well. He asked me if I minded if he called me "Sonny," and I obliged. (What else would a nine- or ten-year-old do?) During the same time, my sister Lonnie nicknamed me "Herbie." I have no idea where that came from!

When attending the beach with the family, I sometimes wore just shorts—no top. Thank God that didn't last long; I soon became uncomfortable with it. After watching the popular *Dance Fever*, I used to pretend I was Denny Terrio. Imagining I was him and acting as the male during sexual fantasies added flame to the fire. When playing house with the kids in the neighborhood I used to pretend I was the husband coming home from work, and my friend, the wife, was cooking. I had some issues with those neighborhood kids too later on. Whenever they saw me, they were out to get me. I used to ride my bike in fear around the block, vigorously ringing the bell when I approached my house so my mother would come out and save me.

Being the shy, quiet one, I was often thought of as a snob at school. I was always left out; I was never called in gym class to be part of any team. I was always the last one, and I never felt like I belonged. I remember in junior high when I was supposed to go to lunch with a group of girls. They didn't wait for me, and I was left sitting by myself at the bus stop, not knowing what to do. I ended up taking the bus back home, safe in the company of my mother. She was surprised to see me, and I told her what happened. She got me a sandwich from a fast food place around the corner. I ate it so fast I almost choked. The only time I was accepted by my peers was when I won the spelling bee in the seventh grade. Back in the classroom the next day, the kids clapped for me then surprised me with a Strawberry Shortcake picture frame that said, "Someone Special."

I did like a few boys at school. I had a crush on one in the second grade and a couple throughout the grammar school years.

I even had one, Dennis, going into high school. I had a picture of us in my locker, slow dancing at my sweet sixteen. *What happened?* Although it is hard to explain, it was just a different kind of like. I knew this for sure when feelings for girls enormously erupted the first few days of attending my all girl high school. The latent homosexual emotions were clearly manifested during this pubescent time. In the beginning, I had a major crush on one very popular and attractive girl, Jill. I was nuts over her. All the feelings that "normal" girls have towards boys, I had towards girls. I was girl crazy instead of boy crazy.

2.
POTENTIAL TREE OF EVIL NURTURED AND MANIFESTED

"It's just a phase," my sisters and mom used to say. "She'll grow out of it." How I hoped it was just a phase too. Of course I wanted to like boys and be "normal" like everyone else. But high school was rough, and feelings of inferiority, not belonging, and unpopularity nourished and deeply embedded these growing feelings. I still was always the quiet one, the one being left out, and this time, being made fun of and laughed at in gym class by the popular girls. At first, I thought they were laughing with me and accepting me, but a little while later I learned the truth.

I remember one of the popular girls lying down while the other stroked her hair. How I longed to be a part of that. I never had any real feminine bonding that I so desperately needed. I never had a "real" or close best friend. I didn't belong to any of the (many) cliques. Most days at lunchtime I ate with the "nerds," and I was considered to be one. When I did eat at a table with a clique (not the popular one by any means), there was always tension; I always felt uncomfortable. It came to the point where I ended up in the library, working and eating lunch with the nun. When I took the bus in the morning, I was apprehensive about seeing a particular clique. Instead of singing the song, "Beat the Clock," by Sparks, I used to sing, "Beat the Clique." As I did in grammar school, I never wanted to ride the bus coming or going with any of the girls or cliques. I didn't belong anywhere.

I was very sensitive growing up; I still am. This could be part of the reason why I developed this condition and not my sisters. I was a different personality type. Things bothered and affected me more at home and with my peers. One day at school, to my surprise, my locker was broken into and some books were stolen. I just couldn't believe it! I was devastated. Plus, I needed my math book (it was my very next class). I didn't know what to do. I explained to my math teacher why I didn't have my book. Thank God, she was nice!

Another day I was in the bathroom stall next to some girls who were smoking. They dropped a lit cigarette by me to pretend it was I who was smoking. Of course, I got in trouble, and I remember sitting in a nun's office trying to defend myself. The icing on the cake was my sweet sixteen, when a group of boys and girls I invited left the party for several hours to go get vodka. I kept wondering when they'd come back. Thank God by the end of the party they did, and everyone got up and danced to the last song, "Point of No Return," by Expose. And I had slow danced with Dennis (that boy I mentioned earlier, whose picture I had hanging in my locker). Although their leaving left a negative impression on me, it wasn't *all* bad.

During my junior year in high school, I went with the school on a trip to Washington, D.C. Christine (part of the regular clique), invited me to stay with her and her friends in the room. The one who was supposed to go ended up not going (it wasn't upon her own volition; I think my going had something to do with it) and lost her deposit of fifty dollars. I think she had

2. POTENTIAL TREE OF EVIL NURTURED AND MANIFESTED

it in for me after that. Anyway, this girl who invited me accepted me, and we became good friends. I still felt like an outcast on that trip though, believe it or not, and I was extremely homesick. But this girl made me feel like I belonged, like I was part of the group. I asked her later on what made her include me, and she said she thought there might be something more to me than what everybody said. She said to herself, *I'm going to give this girl a chance.* Our friendship started from there. She became part of my history. At one time she wanted to purchase "best friend" heart earrings, ones that she and I would both wear. I was ecstatic! Someone considered me their best friend. Wow!

We became too good of friends, and unfortunately I started to have feelings for her—to the degree that I developed a strong emotional dependence on her. Emotional dependency, from what I've learned over the years, is when your emotions depend solely on a person and you cannot be happy without them. Their every action plays on your emotion. It is a very unhealthy way to exist, and it cultivates an emotionally unhealthy relationship. This was my first experience of a relationship like this. Everything was about this girl. I was way too emotionally attached. When she expressed feelings for a boy, I became so filled with jealously and rage that I actually hit her! We didn't speak for a while after that, but being the good person that she was, she forgave me. The friendship didn't last, however. I think it ended because she eventually figured out what was going on with me and that I had feelings for her.

Satan, also known as the "father of lies," works through the mind. He takes psychological defects and plays on them, twisting and turning them so that you fall into sin. In short, he works on your psychological weaknesses. You become ensnared and entrapped by his lies. "Be alert and of sober mind. Your enemy the devil prowls around like a roaring lion looking for someone to devour" (1 Peter 5:8). Because I didn't have proper healthy feminine bonding with my mother as a child, and for other reasons I mentioned in the first chapter, I saw myself as masculine—a bad case of mistaken gender identity. After puberty, because I didn't grow up with close female friends (no feminine bonding with my peers), I "psycho-sexualized" them. The homosexual condition is inherently not about the sex. It is about a need for love, acceptance, and self-esteem. Satan was playing a role in sexualizing the relationships in my already warped mind. This leads to the sin of idolatry: worshipping them as though they were gods.

3.
Branching Out

My college days were the best days of my life. I was the star of my own world. I made new friends, male and female. I experienced a new mode of transportation, new people, thoughts, and ideas. I was involved in many extracurricular activities, mostly writing for the college newspaper and the literary magazine. I went to fraternity parties. I was smart; I graduated with top honors. I experienced Europe on my own for the first time (a senior class trip). As with everything I have a passion for and put my mind to, I threw my whole self into it. Of course, I had my usual peer crushes along the way, and I developed feelings for one of my female professors. She praised me all the time, telling me what a great job I was doing on the school newspaper and sometimes how pretty I looked. (I later found out that she was bisexual.) She was so nice and pleasant—popular with all the students.

When I got a new job at a store in the area during the spring of my sophomore year, I developed a crush on an older female coworker. Nurturing and chubby, she was a mother image for whom I was searching. She was also happy and confident; she was well liked by all the customers.

During my healing process, I realized that the women I "fell" for possessed qualities I didn't see in myself. Such were a sense a humor, popularity, competence, confidence, strength, beauty, security, and "having it all together." However, I realized that although these were qualities I didn't see in myself, these women also possessed similarities to me in terms of appearance: petite, brown hair, and brown eyes. Celebrities, too! One was Tina Fey. This was a symptom of low self-esteem. Since I didn't accept and love myself, I sought it in other women. Now, when I see such a woman on television and elsewhere and I'm tempted, I say to myself, *You are just as beautiful as she is.* And it works! When I told my sister Lonnie (more about her later) this in regard to Tina Fey, she said, "You are *prettier* than she is! She has a big nose!" I thank God for Lonnie. I found this to be true in more cases than not.

College was my age of exploration, just as it is for many young adults. I was confused; I wanted answers. I was tired of living in this "limbo" state. I wanted to know if I was really a lesbian once and for all. *Should I pursue the homosexual lifestyle?* I knew down deep it was against my religion, but since the feelings were so real and intense, I didn't think they were wrong. Either I didn't express them much to my family, or they didn't take them seriously. Soon I joined a homosexual support group at school where I met some others like me. If I remember correctly, the female professor who I had a crush on was the moderator. In some way, I made it known to her that I was reaching out for help, so we went out to lunch one day. Being the liberal that she was, she encouraged me to engage in the lifestyle. She introduced me to the book, *Rubyfruit Jungle*, by Rita Mae Brown. Little did I know it was about lesbianism.

Before long I started seeing some female counselors who pushed me into a homosexual lifestyle as well. I remember one of them asking me, "How long are you going to live in limbo?" Shortly afterwards, I saw an ad in a magazine for "women"

3. BRANCHING OUT

pen pals. It was, of course, for women meeting other women from all around the country. I decided to give it try. So I began surreptitiously writing to a girl in Texas. It went on for quite a while. My family had no idea.

In September 1993, just a few months after my college graduation, I decided to attend a weekend retreat at a Jesuit House in Staten Island, New York. I still could not fully embrace the lesbian or homosexual lifestyle, nor label myself as such. As I look back now, it had to be the Holy Spirit working in me from a time as early on as that. The secular world calls it "conscience," but it was the voice of God muttering deep within me, the soft undertones inside my spirit that prevented me from seeing myself as a lesbian in my mind's eye. But I went to this Jesuit House to search for answers; I went on a quest for the truth. Surely I had to find the solution there, in the mist and serenity of the hills, trees, and nature trails. I loved this place! I had often gone there on high school trips for the day. My mother and Lonnie, acting as chaperones, sometimes accompanied me. So when I found out about this retreat just as I was entering into the adult world, I thought I had finally found the path to confirmation that I was looking for.

While at the Jesuit House, I attended mass and engaged in other activities, but what stood out in my mind was the deep meditation exercise. The nuns would lead us through these guided meditations by using imagery and playing relaxing, spiritual music on a cassette tape recorder. They spoke softly. We would walk through winding valleys and encounter peaceful scenarios until eventually, we met Jesus.

I was "religious" back then, so to speak, in that I totally believed in God, prayed, and went to mass. I was good! I had never partaken in any deviant behavior. No drinking, no drugs. My only issue was this identity confusion. I wrote journals, meditated, and prayed during this retreat. I spent time alone in the woods, contemplating life. We were up early, attending mass and doing spiritual exercises. I made a few friends.

One activity that I remember vividly that was a turning point in my decision to pursue the lesbian lifestyle was a drawing. A group of us sat around a table with a nun who told us to create this drawing that would reveal our inner being or tell us about ourselves, who we were. We drew with colored pencils on 11×14 construction paper. My drawing looked like a flame, although one could interpret it as a monster (turned upside down), or even a vagina, perhaps? I left only with a confirmed sense of my homosexuality.

I continued to explore the lesbian world. The following year, I went back to speak to that nun about the drawing. I figured if she said that homosexuality was okay, the religious aspect would be taken care of and I would have nothing to worry about. She told me that this drawing manifested latent homosexuality. It showed that I was, down deep, indeed a lesbian. Sure enough, she said that God loves us unconditionally just the way we are. She then referred me to a prospective priest from there who would offer me more support. It was so satisfying to me to hear this. I don't remember the reason why she deciphered it as such; she might have persuaded me that it was a vagina or "monster" that was trying to break out from within. Whatever the reason, I was so happy to finally get an answer. This catapulted me deeper into realizing I was going to be part of this lifestyle.

I didn't want to tell my family what had happened at the Jesuit House because I felt they were too old fashioned and narrow minded to understand. They found out anyway, but I refused to listen to them. Lonnie objected the most to it. She didn't believe it. She was aghast when I tried to justify the lifestyle by saying the lie that you could have all the fun you want and not worry about getting pregnant and using birth control. She drove my mother and me back to the retreat house

3. Branching Out

to find this nun and confront her. During the drive over there, I kept taking the nun's side while they were against it. I wanted answers so badly that I was blinded by this nun's deception. Maybe I wanted to hear that it was okay to "be that way" from someone in a religious institution because my feelings were so strong and felt so right and so normal to me. I was hoping inside that my religion would agree with this identity. It was hard to convince my family, though. Whatever Lonnie did or however she found out, that nun who interpreted my drawing was a lesbian herself. Whoa! How deceived I was. She had made up that whole explanation to get me to believe I was a lesbian like she was. Trying to recruit me! As a young, innocent girl probing who I really was, she took advantage of me and tried to trap me. That was the first time that I learned that just because someone wears a religious vestment, they do not always tell the truth.

In early 1994 I actually met a guy, Mickey, at a famous night club in New York City. I always loved to go out dancing. He was nice, handsome, and intelligent. He danced with me and didn't try anything else; he didn't push himself on me like so many other guys did. He didn't even try to kiss me. At the end of the night I gave him my phone number—something I didn't normally do. Even though I didn't feel any sexual attraction to him, I was hoping I would. As I stated earlier, I wanted to be "normal" like everybody else. I *wanted* to like men. We went out a few times, but I didn't get anything out of it. Before the first time we even went out, he sent me flowers on Easter Sunday. My family was all excited, but I felt very nonchalant about it. He wanted to pursue the relationship more than I did, especially on a more physical level. This pushed me even more into the lesbian lifestyle. I knew I had to end it. We remained in contact for a couple of years before we lost touch.

I was so confused. I remembered saying the following prayer almost daily:

> *Dear Lord Jesus, I need you. I can't live the Christian life by myself. When I try to do that, my struggle ends in failure and deceit. I need you to take over my life and live your life through me. I believe that You died on the cross for my sins, and You rose from the dead to bring me new life. I am sorry for all my sins. Please forgive me. I forgive anyone who ever offended me. I open the door of my life and receive You as my Savior and Lord. I turn over my whole life, every detail of my life to You. Take control of my life. Help me to be the kind of person You want me to be. Thank you for forgiving my sins and giving me eternal life. Please send Your Holy Spirit upon me to fill me with love for the Father and for You and to guide and direct me in everything I do and say. I ask this in Your name, Jesus Christ my Lord. Amen.*

Not only did this homosexual aspect of my life perplex me, but I needed a good full-time job. Needless to say, my major, communications, was very competitive. I believe this prayer played a pivotal role in putting me on the right path down the line.

Meanwhile, I was still convinced that lesbianism was the route I was supposed to take. I acted solely on my feelings. I befriended other lesbians and those who were trying to get help "coming out." I found out about a group that met in the city on Friday nights. I went there after work (I had landed a temporary job in the broadcasting field). It was a medium-sized group of women of all ages. They all sat in a circle. The moderator went around the room, and everyone just said what was on their minds. It was sort of like a therapy session. Afterwards we went out for a bite to eat in Chelsea. Sometimes we went to gay clubs in the village. It was fun going out and exploring, being part of this group, feeling accepted. But I was being brainwashed by gay propaganda.

At one point I cut my hair really short and called it "lesbian chic." I even went to Cherry Grove in Fire Island, Long Island, for a day with them. Cherry Grove is a very popular summer destination for gay women of all ages on the south shore of the island. It has restaurants, bars, clubs, and beaches that lesbians frequent. Here, I felt that sense of belonging I so needed. I fit right in! The next town over is Pine Grove (as opposed to Cherry), for gay men. (The night before I went there, I had a big fight with my mother and Lonnie about it. Lonnie was so upset she almost broke her toe.) Most of them stayed overnight or the whole weekend. After leaving, I remember the next day at home feeling so upbeat and positive.

There was one woman about my age who was part of the group. I liked her and wanted to hook up with her. She was the same ethnicity as I was and lived in the same area. Unfortunately she wanted to just be friends with me. As I look back now, I thank God that's all she wanted. I remember seeing her the next day after she spent the weekend with another woman from the group. She expressed how sad and empty she felt when she left. She was like a different person, so dejected. And I realized eventually, that's what this type of relationship does to you. You're so attached and emotionally dependent on the other person that you're lost without them. It's very unhealthy. You're seeking, in that person, the feminine that you don't have in order to complement yourself. You strive and yearn for femininity. When that part of you breaks away for any amount of time, you're lost; you don't know who you are anymore. You fall apart. That's why you become so entangled in each other's lives. That's why there are many rifts in lesbian relationships. And some of them could be violent and deadly. When you perceive that your "other" might leave you or that the relationship is threatened, you break down. An actual article from the *New York Daily News* clearly illustrates this:

Lesbian love spat deadly

A Bronx woman fatally shot her lesbian lover in a rage attack yesterday after the victim said she wanted to end their five-year relationship, Police said. Jeannette Brown fired a single bullet into Sharice Williams' head in their Bronx apartment before turning the gun on herself, police said. Brown, 41, suffered a wound to the stomach and was listed in critical condition last night at Lincoln Hospital, police said. Williams, 34, was pronounced dead at the scene. Investigators recovered two guns in the Grand Concourse apartment and were not immediately certain whether Brown shot herself in a suicide attempt or to make it look like Williams fired at her, a law enforcement source said. "It is such a horrible shock," said a neighbor who identified herself as Gloria. "You'd hear them fight, but you'd never expect anything like this – I thought they were in love." Detectives believe that Williams had told Brown yesterday morning that she was going to leave her, "and that causes her to snap," one investigator said. (*New York Daily News*, Saturday, July 17, 2004)

When in a relationship with someone of the same sex, you experience extreme fits of jealously. Emotionally, you need this

3. Branching Out

person to validate you, to give you the femininity you're searching for, since, according to Leanne Payne in *The Broken Image*, you do not accept it in yourself. She also says that for people who don't believe or who live without a God, the sexual act becomes erotica mania, or another term pertaining to you being the all-powerful one—a no good, unnatural act. The sexual intimacy also becomes an addiction, comparative to animals. You can't live without it. (To verify this, a woman in a lesbian relationship once told me it was like an addiction.) Leanne Payne also says rebellious behavior leads to vengeance and sin, and that when you listen and obey God, your true self shines through gradually; you see yourself through the eyes of God.

That woman from the group and I kept in touch for a while but then drifted apart. A few years later (I'm not sure why God allowed this), my mother and I met her father at a charismatic prayer meeting. He was part of the group, praying for his other daughter who had lupus. We spoke to him as we frequented the weekly meetings for a long while. We never found out if she was still in the lifestyle.

I was becoming hard boiled. I didn't want to listen to my family when they tried to stop me. I think they did preach a little bit to me about the Bible and that homosexuality was sin. They also told me about hell. I didn't want to hear it. I was so deceived by Satan's lies that I didn't believe in hell. I didn't think it existed at all. And I told them that.

Around this time I was still involved with that women's pen pal membership I saw in that magazine. I had stopped writing to that girl in Texas, but I had found someone much closer, in Long Island. We wrote back and forth for a short while before we met. She was older than I was. However, in December 1994, I found myself back at the retreat house with my mother. Again I had the opportunity to talk to that nun, and I was yet under her spell. She was happy with all I was doing. My mother knew what I was up to, but she knew she had no choice with me. However, that day was a turning point in my conversion.

At mass that afternoon, they were administering the sacrament of The Anointing of the Sick. I wasn't sure if I should go up or not. I am ashamed to admit, as a Catholic school girl all my life, I wasn't sure what this sacrament was all about. Something told me to go. I thought I had nothing to lose, so I thought I'd give it a try. As I was in line waiting and watching, I noticed people falling down. I had no idea what was going on. I thought they had fainted or gotten sick. Later, I found out they were being "slain in the spirit." From my understanding, that is when you are so touched by the Holy Spirit and you become filled with Him that you get light-headed while experiencing religious ecstasy and fall on the floor. At some of the healing masses I had gone to they actually had designated "catchers" to catch the people as they fell and gently lay them on the floor until they come to. I realized the falling down was okay since no one seemed to panic or do anything such as call for help or for an ambulance.

We told two women who were slain in the spirit about our situation, and they spoke about hell. That scared me. I went right back to my nun friend and she told me to blow it off, "just like the wind." Of course, that's what I did. Like I said before, I thought I was religious; I believed and loved God and went to church (even though I thought hell didn't exist). I thought this lifestyle was okay, but there was still that voice inside of me that said maybe, just maybe, I was *not* doing the right thing. And, deep down inside, *way deep*, I didn't want to have to live this way. (This might have been one of the reasons I went back to the retreat house.) After receiving this sacrament, God gave me (and my family) these two women that He would work through, and, more importantly, a month later, a change of heart.

Nevertheless, I had recently started seeing my pen pal from Long Island. (In fact, we had our second date the very same day

3. Branching Out

I received the sacrament.) We dated for about six weeks. The last time I saw her I remember calling my house to tell my parents when I'd be home. My father had caught me in a lie. He knew I was at a gay bar. He didn't say anything when I got home, but my whole family was on the warpath. I was warned I'd better stop or I needed to get out of the house. My brother-in-law, Jerry, Lonnie's husband, knew something was going on. He called me one night but I wouldn't listen to him. Soon after he warned Lonnie, "You'd better go talk to your sister." Throughout this whole time she was praying and praying for me. She was praying so hard, she said, that she didn't even know what she was saying. She left a pamphlet on my bed that read, "Dealing with Desires You Cannot Control," by Mark McMinn, with a personal, handwritten note on the inside cover that read,

> *Dear JM,*
>
> *I hope this will help you understand your feelings and deal with them in a Christ like manner rather than giving in to evil. This is just the beginning of our spiritual awakening.*
>
> *Love,*
> *Lonnie*
>
> *P.S. I'm never giving up on you.*

She left another note on top that said, "**JM Urgent**: Read this NOW!" I ignored them.

I didn't even have a full-time job yet, but the very next day I threatened I would move out with my newfound "friend" and cut myself off from the family to go live happily ever after. However, deep down I was fearful, and I wasn't at all happy about what I was doing to my family. Thank God I didn't fully identify myself as a lesbian yet, and calling her my "girlfriend" bothered me.

The thought of two men together also bothered me, although I couldn't understand why. I was living in ambiguity. Just as I was about to go a little deeper into our relationship, the Holy Spirit intervened. I was twenty-three years old.

4.

THE DISCOVERY AND ABSORPTION OF THE LIGHT

The day after Lonnie left the pamphlet on my bed, she wanted to meet and talk with me. *Okay*, I thought. *Now I can really give her a piece of my mind.* We were to spend the day together in Staten Island. I didn't know where she was taking me at first, and I was ill at ease. I was prepared with my books to show her my side of the argument and to prove her wrong. I was ready for battle.

First, she took me to the retreat house to see a priest who explained how homosexual *orientation* is not sin but the *acts* are, and that there is no "end" to homosexuality. I came out with understanding but with nothing else. We then stopped at a beautiful shrine and followed that with a nice, leisurely lunch at an Italian restaurant near the mall. We communicated very calmly and rationally, expressing and understanding each other's side of the story. Lonnie's argument was more powerful than mine. She spoke very compassionately about the wrath of God, how she and the rest of the family loved me, and something to the effect of how they didn't want my soul to suffer eternal damnation. She gave me a book entitled, *How Will I Tell My Mother*, by Jerry Arterburn, that she discovered in a small Christian bookstore in upstate New York.

Ultimately, we came to a sort of compromise. Lonnie asked me to give this (God's way) a try for six months. (Little did I know I would stick with it for twenty years, and counting.) We were going to work through it. I had to trust her. I knew it was the Holy Spirit speaking to me, plus, I liked a challenge.

So, it was on January 16, 1995, when I said yes to the Holy Spirit. It was a dark and dank day; my emotions matched the weather. I came home an emotional wreck. I cried all day and night. I never felt love poured out to me like that before. I was experiencing an inner struggle between the Holy Spirit and Satan's bondage. I knew what lie ahead of me. I felt some regret that it didn't happen sooner, although it happened in the nick of time—God's timing is always perfect. I knew I had to call my "girlfriend" and tell her the news. What turmoil. The next few days I was still in shock that I agreed to this.

By the grace of God, in less than a week, I broke up with two lesbian friends and my "girlfriend." (It is hard for me now to refer to her as such; it is that far removed from me.) Each phone call felt like the hardest thing I ever had to do in my life. Nevertheless, I did feel like a stronger person after each one. I felt good about myself because I was able to do something so difficult.

Another difficult thing I had to do was get rid of all the things I owned that were associated with the lesbian lifestyle. All the books, T-shirts, letters from my pen pals, etc., had to go. I took them all out from under my bed and put them in a black garbage bag while listening to "How Great Thou Art." I was crying because of the loss but also because of the music. What an experience! It was so touching. I thought of God's love and

4. THE DISCOVERY AND ABSORPTION OF THE LIGHT

either grieving my loss or just getting over the past. Thank you, Jesus. "Whoever finds their life will lose it, and whoever loses their life for my sake will find it" (Matthew 10:39).

It was hard for me to totally destroy that bag of memories. I couldn't throw it away just yet. I would, though, and did, eventually! God Bless Lonnie. She held on to it for me until I was ready. She referred to it as "the evil bag." Gay paraphernalia (pictures and posters of women) was replaced with religious paraphernalia (those of Jesus and Mary, as well as religious sayings, crosses, calendars, and Bible quotes). Disconnecting with the people and things is extremely important. We have to let go of all the evil—all the dirt, filth, dust, and cobwebs in our house so Jesus can come in and work. Otherwise, as one priest said, "He feels uncomfortable." You have to have a clean slate.

During the next few weeks, we went to prayer meetings, spoke to the women who were slain in the spirit I met at the retreat house, and visited Jesus in a Perpetual Adoration Chapel, or Blessed Sacrament, for the first time. I wrote down and studied relevant Bible quotes and put more effort into saying the rosary correctly. Here are some of the quotes that I meditated on daily that helped me tremendously:

> *Trust in the Lord with all thine heart; and lean not into thine own understanding. In all thy ways acknowledge Him, and He will direct thy paths. (Psalm 3:5-6)*
>
> *Choosing rather to suffer affliction with the people of God, than to enjoy the pleasures of sin for a season. (Hebrews 11:25)*
>
> *Cast thy burden upon the Lord, and he shall sustain thee: he shall never suffer the righteous to be moved. (Psalm 55:22)*
>
> *These things I have spoken unto you, that in me ye might have peace. In the world ye shall have tribulation: but be of good cheer; I have overcome the world. (John 16:33)*

Consider it pure joy, my brothers, when you face trials of many kinds, because you know that the testing of your faith develops perseverance. Perseverance must finish its work so that you may be mature and complete, not lacking anything. (James 1:2-4)

Blessed is the man who perseveres under trial because, having stood the test, that person will receive the crown of life that the Lord has promised to those who love him. (James 1:12)

I can do all things through Christ who strengthens me. (Philippians 4:13)

Now the body is not for sexual immorality but for the Lord, and the Lord for the body....Do you not know that your bodies are members of Christ? Flee sexual immorality. Every sin that a man does is outside the body, but he who commits sexual immorality sins against his own body. Or do you not know that your body is the temple of the Holy Spirit who is in you, whom you have from God, and you are not your own? For you were bought with a price; therefore glorify God in your body. (1 Corinthians 6:13-20)

Be anxious for nothing, but in everything by prayer and supplication, with thanksgiving, let your requests be made known to God; and the peace of God, which surpasses all understanding, will guard your hearts and minds through Christ Jesus. (Philippians 4:6-7)

Therefore, that I might not become too elated, a thorn in the flesh was given to me, an angel of Satan, to beat me, to keep me from being too elated. Three times I begged the Lord about this, that it might leave me, but he said to me, "My grace is sufficient for you, for power is made perfect in weakness! I would rather boast most gladly of my weaknesses, in order that the power of Christ may dwell with me. Therefore, I

4. THE DISCOVERY AND ABSORPTION OF THE LIGHT

am content with weaknesses, insults, hardships, persecutions, and constraints, for the sake of Christ; for when I am weak, then I am strong." (2 Corinthians 12:7-10)

Because he has set his love upon Me, therefore I will deliver him; I will set him on high, because he has known my name. He shall call upon Me, and I will answer him; I will be with him in trouble; I will deliver him and honor him. With long life I will satisfy him, And show him My salvation. (Psalm 91:14-16)

I also went to meetings with Lonnie to meet others in the same situation as we were. We visited a couple who were members of Encourage (a support group for parents with children dealing with SSA) who helped their daughter out of the lifestyle. The father's family history of both generations almost paralleled ours! He gave us a lot of reassurance that we weren't alone. He sat and spoke with us about what the Bible said about homosexuality. Then he explained how his daughter was very colicky as a baby and he didn't allow his wife to pick her up when she cried. He believed this was the major cause of her homosexuality. That was the main thing that stuck with me during that visit. It is another example of a lack of feminine bonding during the early stages of development.

After that, we revisited the priest at the retreat house. We learned about healing masses and other prayer meetings (one charismatic) being held. Lonnie had been getting testimonials in the mail from people in upstate New York who belonged to organizations and ministries that transformed them through Jesus Christ. We were inundated with telephone numbers, books, and pamphlets to read. Two such were, "Emotional Dependency," by Lori Rentzel, and "Homosexual Struggle." So much happened in the ensuing weeks. I even went to speak to my philosophy professor who I admired so much at my college. He, along with the priest at the retreat house, advised me to read St. Paul's first letter to the Corinthians on love in the Bible. He also provided me with the following insight:

- Sexual desire is the most powerful of all desires.
- Homosexuality is morally wrong across all doctrines, not just Christianity.
- Something cannot be good if we can't teach it to our children.
- God's love for us is eternal, not temporal.
- The adulterous relationships/affairs in the world and literature are the most rapturous and full of elation. (Just like I heard women say: their encounters with women were nothing they've ever experienced with men because they are sinful and there is so much pleasure in sin.)
- Intelligent people suffer more.

Here's the understanding I gained in that short period of time:

- Temptation is God's way of getting us closer to Him.
- We are tempted by Satan (if all of this were true) for hours after we go out of our way for God.
- This was going to make me a stronger and more responsible person.
- Life is difficult; there will always be struggles, and everyone has his own strife.
- God loves me, but He loves me too much to leave me where I was. He had a better plan for my life.
- The lifestyle is glamorous and exciting now but won't be twenty or thirty years from now.
- You have to manage temptation, not deny it.

4. The Discovery and Absorption of the Light

- Jesus gives us crosses to bear to be more like Him.
- The reason why so many lesbians say they "came out" after college or graduate school was because of idol minds and the devil's work. Because their minds were so busy with school, they didn't have time for this deviousness. They claim they just put aside this important aspect of their lives for exploration later on.
- The reason why this and all other sinful relationships fall apart is because they are not based on truth. No foundation. A falsehood.
- The relationship is like a fake diamond: when you see it, it looks great, but after you have it, it's phony and it cuts you up.
- From *Coming Out of Homosexuality*, by Bob Davies and Lori Rentzel, lustful fantasies are sinful, temptations and orientation are not. Continued sinful thoughts are sinful, because they lead you to act on them. This makes sense because thoughts lead to actions and actions lead to habits. It is also in accordance with Proverbs 23:7, "As he thinks in his heart, so he is."
- Also from Davies and Rentzel's book, the relationships are not satisfying in their "end"; they're like drinking salted water—you always thirst for more.

It was scary to me that all of this made sense. The main reason why I decided to stick to "God's way" for my life was because I believed that Lonnie was a messenger from God and caught me at the perfect time: God's time. And the prayers for my life that I had been praying for over a year had been answered: God's plan for my life. God said there was a better way. I had gotten just a taste of the lifestyle, and God stopped it before it got too far. If it had happened any sooner or later, things might not have worked out as they did. I still missed my old "girlfriend" and was tempted to call her. I secretly hoped that this was all a farce and that I would go back to her someday, and maybe they would prove that it was biological after all. As much as a struggle and as miserable as I was, I knew I couldn't give in.

I recognized that the changes in my thinking and behavior were very subtle and gradual. I knew it was Jesus' work and not coincidence. It was really sinking in, and I thanked Jesus more and more. I was slowly maturing. I thought I was doing very well, but I was afraid to get my hopes up for fear the temptation would come back; but with Christ, I had nothing to fear. "Fear not, for I am with you. Do not be dismayed. I am your God. I will strengthen you; I will help you; I will uphold you with my victorious right hand" (Isaiah 41:10).

5.
Gradually Growing Into Good

My prayer meetings kept me going, learning more and more about Jesus and the Bible, as did my rosaries and visits to the Blessed Sacrament—it is here that you experience the true presence and love of Jesus in the Eucharist. It is here that you see yourself in the "Divine Image," the way your Creator sees you; in turn, it increases your self-esteem and self-image. (The more you spend time with someone too, the more you become like them.) The woman from Encourage told me to just sit and feel the love of Jesus—to let Him love you—and oh, how healing it was. She explained that it is like the rays of the sun. You may not feel the impact at first, but eventually you're going to see the results.

I chose Mary, the mother of Jesus, to be my role model of what it means to be a woman. Mary is the epitome of femininity for me because she is the "new Eve," as she crushed that evil serpent with her foot. She was not afraid to follow God's will when she said yes to the angel Gabriel to be the mother of Jesus.

"And Mary said, 'Behold, the bondslave of the Lord; may it be done to me according to your word.' And the angel departed from her" (Luke 1:38). When Jesus then saw His mother and the disciple whom He loved standing nearby, He said to His mother, "Woman, behold, your son!" Then He said to the disciple, "Behold, your mother!" From that hour, the disciple took her into his own household (John 19:26).

I tried to follow A.C.T.S. when I prayed: I first started with praise and *adoration*, then I *confessed*, then I *thanked* Jesus for everything and the present day, and then I *supplicated*. I prayed for Him to keep up the faith and courage in me and to keep taking me every step of the way. I prayed for emotional healing. I asked Him to fill my desires with His plans for my life, to help me have healthy relationships (which is most important to Him), and to denounce the false inner vows I had about men. (I learned that hatred of the opposite sex is a sin.) From one of my prayer meetings, I learned to say the following (and others prayed this over me):

> *Give me a hedge of protection so high so the fiery darts of the enemy can't get through, and a spiritual ring of fire from the top of my head to the souls of my feet (because Satan is like a prowling lion ready to devour). Heal me in every way that needs to be healed. Wash me of my iniquities. Keep me holy and sanctified before You.*

I started to use oil on my forehead, and I obtained scapulars. A little later on, I learned the Chaplet of Divine Mercy. I went to mass and received Communion as often as I could, and more frequently I received the sacrament of confession. These, combined with visiting the Blessed Sacrament and saying the rosary are what significantly changed me. Jesus changed me.

I researched local church activities and thought about joining the choir. I continued to receive mailings and newsletters

5. Gradually Growing Into Good

from ministries and kept in contact with others who successfully left the lifestyle. I constantly listened to a Bible station called "Family Radio." I listened to songs of praise and healing on cassette tapes as well as the book of Ephesians. I absorbed teachings of preachers on the prayer channels and recorded them on cassettes. I kept in touch with other Christians I met at the meetings and continued going to masses once a month where worshippers were being slain in the spirit. At the charismatic prayer meetings, I was prayed over. I spoke out at support meetings. I continued to read testimonies and spiritual books as well as books on healing.

Later on in the 2000s, I learned the truth about sexuality on CD from Christopher West's interpretation of Pope John Paul's [the second] *Theology of the Body*. I learned and accepted the fact that one is not born homosexual. It was quickly revealed to me that Simon LeVay's studies and alleged "proof" that sexual orientation is genetic because of differences in brain structures of heterosexuals and homosexuals was wrong. (I just learned he is gay himself. That doesn't surprise me.)

It was nice not to be confused anymore. Eventually, I started to "see" for the first time that two women cannot and are not made to live together as one. They're too similar; they'd clash! I "saw" the complementariness between men and women. I was very cognizant of what I watched on television and movies and what I read in books and magazines (I still am). Basically, I was building up spiritual walls against the enemy. "Submit yourselves, then, to God. Resist the devil, and he will flee from you. Draw near to God, and He will draw near to you" (James 4:7-8).

Lonnie was my trusted source of constant support: my accountability. We met on a regular basis to talk about my progress and breakthroughs. We discussed male "models," so to speak. We acknowledged and made a list of "good" men we knew—men that provided great examples and ones I could possibly like. We analyzed the information in books together to get to the root of the problem. One that made the greatest impact on us was one that I mentioned a few times before: *Homosexuality: A New Christian Ethic,* by Elizabeth Moberly. It was here that we first heard the term and learned about *defensive detachment*, which claims that one root cause of homosexuality is a result of a deficit with the same-sex parent. This made perfect sense to us, as I explained earlier. Throughout the years and to this day, I've see many cases like this, especially in males. In families where the son is living a gay lifestyle, the mother was the loud, domineering, overbearing figure, and the father was the quiet, submissive, wimpy one: the doormat. It was also from this book that we learned how being too over-protective could be detrimental. These were major discoveries for us in the healing process.

Lonnie also accompanied me to the prayer meetings and healing masses. One day when she came with me to a Courage Day of Recollection at St. John's Parish House, somebody told me how blessed I was to have Lonnie. Lonnie replied, "I'm blessed, too." At one point I thought about resisting the whole thing because I thought I had to feel heterosexuality; I thought the purpose was to get married. Lonnie made it clear when she said, "I don't care if you never get married. I just don't want you to suffer eternally." That was a relief! And of course, I called her during my down and tempting times—there were still plenty of them. I probably would have given up if it weren't for Lonnie.

My "real" struggle lasted about a year to a year and six months. By "real" struggle I mean days when many tears were shed and when I wanted to give up, thinking I would never get over it. There were days when I still yearned to be with a woman; days when I missed and still yearned to be with the "friend" I dated for six weeks; days when I felt utter hopelessness. There were nights when I thought I would never admire a man's voice over a woman's. One night in particular, I had a major temptation to call "her." It was 10:30 p.m. I was crying and wailing because I couldn't call her, so I called Lonnie and that made me feel better.

5. Gradually Growing Into Good

Then I went outside in my backyard under a tree and fell down on my knees. I looked up at the sky and spoke honestly to God, saying, "Why, God, Why?" as I poured out my feelings. I learned that our past is Jesus' present—that God's time is always now. To Him, our hurts are now. After this experience outside with God, I felt much better.

That event happened the same day I attended the Courage Day of Recollection. That day, I learned we should stumble and fall into heaven rather than slide into hell. This is exactly what Jesus tells us to do in Matthew 7:13: "Go in through the narrow gate, because the gate is wide and the road is spacious that leads to destruction, and many people are entering by it." I learned that the theme song of hell was, "I Did It My Way," by Frank Sinatra. When you take the narrow road, or I like to refer to it as "The Road Not Taken" (a poem by Robert Frost), you gain wisdom and understanding, which was exactly what happened to me. "Get wisdom; get insight; do not forget, and do not turn away from the words of my mouth" (Proverbs 4:5).

That day, I had also interacted with other members and spoke to the director (at that time, it was Fr. Harvey, God rest his soul) who said he might use my testimony in his book. I received confession and Communion. And yet, Satan certainly tried to get me that night! After I was on a "high" and very close to God, he tried to tempt me. As admirable preacher Joyce Meyer says, "New level, new devil." He attacks when you reach a new level in your relationship with God.

Lots of people said that my year to a year and six month struggle was a short time. And it was then that I was set free. "So if the Son sets you free, you will be free indeed" (John 8:36). Don't get me wrong, the temptations and healing process were ongoing. I am talking about not being controlled and ensnared by it. Not being a slave to your emotions or passions. When something is no longer a secret and brought out into the light, it no longer entraps or has power over you. I learned the truth and it literally has set me free. "Then you will know the truth, and the truth shall set you free" (John 8:32).

God allows some people to suffer more than others. He knows how much each person can take and all they need individually for His greater glory. "There hath no temptation taken you but such as is common to man: but God is faithful, who will not suffer you to be tempted above that ye are able; but with the temptation also make a way to escape, that ye may be able to bear it" (1 Corinthians 10:13).

Another quote that comforted me was 2 Corinthians 4:17: "For this momentary, light affliction is producing for us an eternal weight of glory beyond all comparison." And I often prayed, "Let Your will be done, not mine." To get *to* you have to go *through*. We came from God and we are going to God. We are on the road, travelling. As Joyce Meyer once said, in order to get from the pit to the palace, you have to go through the middle. As I learned in *Homosexual No More*, by Dr. William Consiglio, suffering and going through trials gives us inner strength and raises our self-esteem in the long haul. It was my lack of self-esteem that brought SSA on in the first place. This is where James 1:2-4 comes into play.

Another encouraging thought that I learned was to look at what you can achieve, not at your limitations. Let's not forget, "And we know that all things work together for good to them that love God, to them who are the called according to his purpose" (Romans 8:28). I liked the way Fr. Jim Andrews explained it on Family Radio's program, "Don't Worry, Be Happy." Firstly, God wants to have happiness, but not transient happiness that sinful acts and material goods bring. He wants us to have a holy happiness—His purpose is to make us like Christ (to suffer here on earth first). Secondly, God reveals His sovereignty in that "all things work together." Think of it like the ingredients that make up a pie: flour, evaporated milk, and sugar, for example. But, if you use them individually, you might think, "Oh, no!" But, if you

5. GRADUALLY GROWING INTO GOOD

mix them together under the right temperature, they become a masterpiece in the long run.

One of the Woman's Courage meetings Lonnie and I attended was located right past a gay club I went to where I had my first kiss with my "girlfriend." The Holy Spirit is surely always with us; He is with us even when He does not like what we are doing (sinning). I witnessed this firsthand because when I was there, I could not even look at myself in the mirror in the bathroom. I knew I was being convicted by the Holy Spirit. Anyway, I was nervous as we drove by the club. When we did, I said "goodbye" twice, and then I got slightly teary-eyed. The feeling went away.

As we passed it again on the way back (we had no choice), I kept saying, "Jesus is with me." I prayed for the courage to pass it. Lonnie said that Jesus must have been crying when I was in there. Then I said, "Out with the old—that was my past life." Then we realized that of course, it was put there for a reason. This occurred to me the day after the sermon on temptation when the priest said, "Don't be afraid of him (Satan). Use Jesus' words, 'Man shall not live on bread alone, but on every word that comes out of the mouth of God'" (Matthew 4:4.) It wasn't a coincidence. It didn't affect me as much on the way back.

The meeting had gone well. The women were nice. We listened to a cassette tape from a lecturer and one woman lent it to me to record it. I was glad. I wanted to go back. Later, Lonnie and I were talking about how that lecturer was going to be me someday. After that, I went alone to the meetings sometimes. By the third time, I was hardly tempted by the club. On the way back one night, I actually thanked Jesus for "getting me out of that hellhole."

Another instance was when I was returning home from Boston with my other sister, Marissa. We were traveling in a cab through the city from Penn Station. Sure enough, we passed a lesbian night club I used to go to. Marissa told me to close my eyes. I did it for a few seconds and then I stopped. I said (not sure if out loud or to myself), "No, I'm not going to do this. It's not right. I'm not closing my eyes to the world. Jesus didn't do that!" When I opened them, they laid right on the club. What a challenge, I thought. Again, I kept reciting Jesus' words, "Man shall not live on bread alone, but on every word that comes out of the mouth of God" (Matthew 4.4), and "Greater is He who is in me than is in the world" (1 John 4:4). It passed. We drove by and it was over. Complete. Done. Thank you, Jesus. I hardly felt emotional that time.

I had a lot of issues to resolve. I had to forgive my parents and my past schoolmates. Of course, that is a process, and it is probably still going on. I had a lot of anger towards my father. It was probably because of the way he treated my mother and the negative things she embedded in my mind about him when I was growing up. Maybe it was because he didn't act like the father I wanted to have. When he did something to upset me, I gave my anger to Jesus and prayed to Him to help me let go of it. I constantly prayed to Him to help me and I got over it. Then, in one instance, I put on a healing tape. It was in the times that I was upset with my father and not able to speak my mind and be honest with him that I wanted to give up. This fed my already low self-esteem, one of the symptoms of SSA. On good days with him I was in a good mood and wasn't tempted.

One Sunday after we all went out to breakfast, I drove home alone with him while my mother and Marissa walked. We spoke about the car. He told me what oil was good for the engine. Then, he offered to take me to buy the oil! I couldn't because I had to meet Lonnie at the 12:30 p.m. mass. After I dropped him off at home and got out of the car and walked to church, I felt really good. I realized again the correlation between my lack of bitterness and anger toward my father and not feeling tempted to sin. Sin breeds sin. After that incident, I wanted to spend more time with him. I thanked Jesus for answering my

5. Gradually Growing Into Good

prayers as I had been praying fervently for a desire to get to know him. I believed I had to do that first before I my desire to know men would develop. Soon, I didn't want to call him by the negative nickname my mother made up for him. I learned early on that my relationship to him was a major part of the problem that needed healing.

I had to forgive my mother, too, for the resentment she filtered in my mind about my father. I absorbed it like a sponge as any prepubescent would. I had an innate anger towards men. What helped me the most in this area was when Jesus said to God the Father when He was dying on the cross, referring to His crucifiers, "Forgive them, for they know not what they do." This helped me forgive my schoolmates too. The more you receive the love of God, the easier it is to forgive. You want to do what He says. I learned that you have to let go of expectations from your parents. They are overgrown children and ordinary people with hurts just like you, they're just older. You have to take them off their pedestal. You have to realize they are human and they make mistakes too.

Jesus works through sorrow. He doesn't work through anger or unforgiveness. He told me to grieve. I had to relive some of the experiences that caused me pain. Remember, in order to get *to*, you have to go *through*. I remember one day I cried for that young child in the first grade (myself) who was so overprotected by her mother, who cried and vomited in the classroom sink most mornings, and who felt rejected by her peers. I cried for the young girl who was brainwashed against her father and for it having to happen that way. One day I asked Jesus, "What went wrong in my relationship with my mother?" I was so overprotected by her that I looked to other women for that same protection as an adult—an extension for my mother's protection. I got an overabundance of it from her and felt none from my father. That's another reason why I was attracted to older, buxom, nurturing women: the mother images. I never felt protection from a man.

Easter fell on the three month anniversary of my being saved: April 16, 1995. It wasn't a coincidence! I was happy in my relationship with Jesus. Marissa and I had gone to the Vigil mass Saturday night. I was so glad I went. It was the first time in my life I actually looked forward to that time of year. I really wanted to go to renew my Baptismal Rites. I was really into it; I meant every word. I had a wonderful Easter Sunday. The Lord provided a beautiful sunny day.

On our drive back from Lonnie's house that day, the Holy Spirit brought up a memory from my past that needed healing. He needed to show me the truth about my mother's pregnancy with me—that she was happy to have a third child. My mother said something to my aunt that made be believe I was unwanted. The circumstances surrounding my birth were still bothering me. I had a sense of being unloved; I felt so worthless, like nothing, like I really didn't belong. Sometimes, I wished I was never born. I thought I had confronted her about this prior to 1995, but apparently we didn't get to the root. I cried a little on the way home, and Marissa comforted me. She reminded me that the doctor gave my parents the option to have an abortion, but they wouldn't even think of it! And she told me how glad she was that that didn't happen!

When I got home, I let my inner child's feelings surface. I spoke about how unworthy I felt. I learned you have to name it, feel it, talk about it, and act. So, I decided to pro-act instead of react. I had to confront my mother about this when the Holy Spirit told me the right time. You have to face painful memories and open up the lines of communication so the Holy Spirit can heal them. Of course I spoke to Lonnie about this and she agreed. I had to know I was wanted. When you are young you perceive things so literally and take things your parents say so seriously, especially as such a sensitive kid as I was.

5. Gradually Growing Into Good

About a week later when I asked my mother about it, I was crying a little and nervous. She took it lightly (now I realize she's right) and told me how glad she was that she didn't have a tumor (because that's what the doctor said it could be)! She also said it was good to have another child. She was excited to see who it would look like. At first she thought she was too old (forty going on forty-one), but then she was happy because it brought the family closer. We hugged after that, but I sensed only a bit of relief. Because of all those years of wrong thinking and being insecure (what a waste!), I still needed time for it to sink in.

Lonnie told me how proud my father was. Then she told me something in my past led me to grieve over what should have been. She said when I was in the hospital, my father cried while looking at me through the window. He hid this from the rest of the family. This evoked such a deep sorrow in me. Every time I heard of his love for me like that I got so melancholy; I grieved over our lost relationship—all the years I missed because of false perceptions of him (from myself and my mother). Lonnie understood this. That night, I cried for the girl who grew up "without" a father. I sobbed for not being the daughter to him I should have been.

As I looked at Jesus' Divine Mercy picture (Jesus, I trust in you), He allowed me to grieve more. I said to myself, *I'm sorry. I forgive you for not being the father I expected you to be, due to your own childhood traumas and my false perceptions. I'm sorry, "Dad."* Dad! I called him "Dad." Like I mentioned before, I never said the word to his face. I was surprised that word came out of my mouth. He would've been so happy to hear me call him that. I prayed that Jesus would restore our relationship. The Lord knew I wanted to have a relationship with him before it was too late. I prayed for the right opportunity for confrontation and conversation to take place. I left it to the Lord. I thanked Him for bringing me this far. I knew I couldn't rush this. There was more to come. I felt somewhat relieved, but the Lord told me there was more to go. I thanked Jesus that this happened only three months to the date of my salvation.

I practiced the "forgiveness method" on my parents, especially my father. I had it up on my bedroom wall for a long time:

1. "In the Name of Jesus, I bind Satan from putting me back into bitterness and unforgiveness."

2. "I have chosen to forgive my parents (father) and I reaffirm that choice right now."

3. "Lord, I bring you this incident…" (Express feelings, be specific.)

4. "Lord, I pray for my father. Help him to prosper spiritually; draw him closer to You each day."

Please be aware that this is a process. You have to say these things every time you experience a resentful thought.

If you really were rejected by your parents, don't despair. God is your heavenly Father, and He loves you! God wants you: "For my father and my mother have forsaken me, but the Lord will take me up" (Psalm 27:10). He chose you before the world began: "For he chose us in him before the creation of the world to be holy and blameless in his sight" (Ephesians 1:4). You are His masterpiece: "For we are God's masterpiece, created in the Messiah Jesus…" (Ephesians 2:10). He has you carved in the palm of His hand: "Behold, I have engraved you on the palms of my hands…" (Isaiah 49:16). As He says in Psalm 139:13-16, "For you created my inmost being; you knitted me together in my mother's womb. I praise you, for I am fearfully and wonderfully made. Wonderful are your works; my soul knows it very well. My frame was not hidden from you, when I was being made in secret, intricately woven in the depths of the earth. Your eyes saw my unformed substance; in your book were written, every one of them, the days that were formed for me, when as yet

5. Gradually Growing Into Good

there was none of them." I read this over and over every night in the beginning stages of my healing process. That same woman from Encourage told me that God does a special work through these verses. I often prayed before I left the Blessed Sacrament, "Thank You for creating me a woman. Thank You for making me Your daughter."

At that point, I was a baby Christian. I was in the beginning stages; I was absorbing all the milk. I was on a honeymoon with Jesus. The new relationship was so exciting. Things were happening so rapidly. I was truly in a state of grace. One day after mass, I was sitting in front of the Blessed Sacrament for a while and knelt down. The sun hit it in such a way that the borders turned bright gold. I knew it was Jesus communicating to me. One night during the prayer meeting when a leader was instituting the sacrament of Communion, for a moment I saw something that appeared like the outline of Jesus' face in the Holy Eucharist! Then it was gone. It seemed surreal . . . but in that moment, I felt like God was encouraging me.

I used to feel the presence of God at night when I closed my eyes and went to sleep. One night as I lie in bed, I prayed, "Cover me with your precious blood," and "Thank you, Jesus." I really felt His presence. I can't describe what happened to my body during those moments; it was a light, levitating sensation. It felt like a surge of power or electricity. After feeling it for a second, I actually got nervous! I said thank you to Jesus for revealing His presence to me.

I also used to see colorful, blue visions when I closed my eyes. They gradually emerged, not quite round, with yellow borders around them. I felt peace. I knew it was Jesus. One time while I was in the semi-conscious or alpha state, I had a "bad" thought and was about to perform a homosexual act. I was fighting so hard to stop it but I couldn't. Then, very quickly, I saw bright green rings with blue in the middle. Jesus! And on another night, while I lie in bed, I said to myself, *Jesus, I love you*, seven times (God's divine number). I felt His presence yet again—that light, indescribable feeling.

One night in March of the same year (1995), I saw a vision. I was rushing to my car to go to a Bible meeting when I casually glanced upon the vacant lot next door to my house. Dead center, I saw a baby about one to two years old in an umbrella stroller facing me. The baby was a boy with dark hair, wearing an orange jacket. I did not see anybody come out of the lot, and as I got in the car, Marissa was walking home from the bus stop. She saw just me—nobody else walking down the block or crossing the street with a carriage. In fact, she said it was pretty desolate. I didn't see anybody walking around the corner, either. When my mother walked through the lot to my car, she saw nothing. I don't think I heard the baby, but he might have been moving his arms up and down. To me, it was a vision of my future, that I would marry a man and have a baby someday. I prayed and thought about the orange silk jacket Lonnie had recently bought me. (It was no coincidence that both jackets were orange.) When I told her about the vision, she got so excited and later referred to it during her times of support. I thanked Jesus profusely and prayed for more visions. It was a clear night, and it happened just as Satan was trying to make us late for the Bible meeting. I haven't received any more visions since then, but in retrospect, I think the baby was me; maybe I still "saw" myself as a boy, and Jesus was physically showing me that I was a baby and alive in Him.

I continued to learn about the blood of Jesus and how powerful it was. I used to say, "There's power in the blood of Jesus," and, "Cleanse me with Your precious blood." This helped me in times of temptation. I remember fairly recently, lying in bed and getting ready to go to sleep when a "bad" thought about a woman started to enter my mind. (Drifting off to sleep is a major temptation time. More on that later.) I said, "Jesus, cleanse my mind with Your precious blood." He did! The thought

5. Gradually Growing Into Good

disappeared. Also, it can be as simple as saying, "Jesus, help me." You don't have to think of all these fancy words and phrases.

A major significant truth God revealed to me was the truth about Creation. It was 10 p.m. on Monday, December 26, 1983. I was a very impressionable twelve year old. I was lying on the couch in the living room with my family and we were deciding what to watch on television. I wanted to watch something educational. At that time in television history there was still nothing good on! Marissa suggested a show on a local PBS station entitled, "The Making of Mankind." Not having any idea what it was about, although it sounded good, I told her to put it on. It opened immediately with a moving image of the progression of ape to man, or the "ascent of man." It scared the living daylights out of me. We changed the channel right away. Nonetheless, it haunted me for years. Twelve years, to be exact.

To think that we all came from apes? How horrible! Every time I looked at another person, I thought they were inherently apes and not the humans as I understood them to be. By the age of twelve, I always thought, in the simple way a child could, from what I learned from my family and in my very early years of Catholic school, that God created us uniquely and individually. This was the first time I heard about *this*. (By the way, evolution was being taught in my sixth grade class!) What I knew up until then, my whole foundation, was shattered. I was traumatized. I drove my family crazy, and I couldn't sleep for weeks. They told me it was just a theory, but I couldn't shake that image from my mind.

When I was around seventeen, we had a house call from a doctor. It still affected me so much that my mom asked the doctor about it. When she referred to it as a theory, he said, "It's not a theory, it's a fact." Then he suggested I read a book called, *From Fish to Philosopher*. That's all I needed to hear! Needless to say, I continued to grapple with this issue. I literally had a fear of evolution. I avoided perusing through my biology textbook my freshman year of high school. I avoided science classes in college. In one of my honors seminars, we were required to read Darwin's *Origin of Species* and write a reaction paper on it. I'm not sure if or how I wormed my way out of that one! I couldn't look at apes or monkeys. I was selective about what I watched on TV—no science shows or shows that were based on evolution. (I still don't watch them because I don't agree with them now.) It was a terrible way to live.

A revelation came to me as I continued to listen to Family Radio during the spring of 1995. It was on that station that I first heard about ICR, The Institute of Creation Research. I contacted them right away and started receiving their newsletter, "Acts and Facts," on a regular basis. (I still have all of them.) I was learning the truth about God's literal six days of Creation. I listened to their broadcasts and announcements pertaining to Creation facts on Family Radio. Then I learned about the Bible Science Association and Answers in Genesis. Soon I found out there was a Creation magazine! How God was inundating me all at once with this truth! When you submit yourself to God's will and obey Him, it's amazing at what He can and will do.

Joshua told the people, "Consecrate yourselves, for tomorrow the LORD will do amazing things among you" (Joshua 3:5). I know that God had to reveal this to me also because He had to show me that all of His Word was true and could be trusted. That's why I had trouble fully embracing that lesbianism was a sin and believing the Bible. I had been praying to Jesus for this. I said, "Please, Lord Jesus, show me the right time. Give me the right opportunity to tackle this according to your will and time. Show me which areas to tackle first. Let your Spirit lead me to true belief in the Creation story." How could I believe and live by what it said about homosexuality if I wasn't sure what it said about Creation? How could I trust how Jesus felt about same-sex relationships if I didn't trust what He said about the beginning of the world? Everything was tying in together. It was truly amazing.

What I learned, too, was that homosexuality is a fruit of evolutionary thinking. If we weren't created male and female by God and in the image of God and were here by random chance as a mere product of evolution, then being intimate with members of the same sex would be perfectly fine. We would just exist as products of particles coming together haphazardly, or just like animals with no conscience, free to do whatever we want and be whatever we want. There would be absolutely no reason to believe that homosexuality is wrong.

I started to order books and cassette tapes from all the organizations on different aspects of creationism. It all made perfect sense! I learned about all the scientific fallacies of evolution and how God's Creation is more credible. There is more proof of intelligent design than random occurrences. In fact, I wrote my master's thesis, "World Views of Creation," on how all the ancient myths of Creation point to the one true one: the biblical Christian account in Genesis. I even thought about becoming a Creation scientist. (I still do!) And through all of this discovery, a burden was lifted from me. I was finally free from this fear of evolving from apes.

I can't emphasize John 8:32 enough: "And you will know the truth, and the truth will make you free." Had I pursued the lesbian lifestyle, I would have probably lived with this nightmare for the rest of my life. I am not afraid to look at primates anymore. The "ascent of man" still bothers me, but I know it is all fabrication. It doesn't affect me at all in the way it used to. I thank Jesus all the time for showing me this truth.

In October 1998, I brought Marissa to a weekend seminar ICR had in Ocean City, New Jersey. Once a believer in evolution from all she was taught in school (Catholic schools like I attended, nevertheless), she was now convinced that God's account of Creation and a young earth is true.

During the summer of 1995, I attended the annual Courage Conference in the Bronx. I had mixed emotions when I arrived. At first, I said to myself, *What am I doing here?* and felt the urge to fight off tears. But then I saw some familiar faces and felt better. It was a good and well-spent weekend. I already knew most of the things the speakers said, but some articulated and rephrased the ideas in such a way that they were absorbed in a new light. I learned that we don't trust ourselves to find our home in our heart; we have an address but are never there. We find ourselves everywhere else but where Jesus Christ is. To Him, relationships are a mosaic or myriad. To us, they're a dyad. And, when we sit face-to-face with the Lord, He is transforming us.

I also learned of a holistic approach from 1969 called the "Psychophysiological Principle." This stated, "Every change in the physiological state is accompanied by an appropriate change in the mental-emotional state, conscious or unconscious; and, conversely, every change in the mental-emotional state, conscious or unconscious, is accompanied by an appropriate change in the physiological state." The testimonials comforted me. One statement one woman said that I liked was, "If you're afraid to do something, do it scared." Well, that means *courage*.

I had the pleasure of meeting Fr. Benedict Groeschel, C.F.R. The thing that stood out in my mind above everything else he said was, "It is truly a mystery that you are here." I brought home some religious books from the conference. That night, I felt down and tempted again, even tempted by that woman who gave the testimonial! I was suffering from feelings of low self-esteem. At dinnertime, I was feeling the pain of brokenness and unexpressed feelings. I hated the tension. I went upstairs and cried in my bedroom. I asked again, *Why me?* Remember "new level, new devil." I kept thinking, *Don't be discouraged; don't give up!*

That night, I got in my car and sped to the Perpetual Adoration Chapel. It was like going to the emergency room for a physical ailment. Instead, I had a deep emotional and spiritual

5. GRADUALLY GROWING INTO GOOD

ailment. You have ongoing appointments with your doctor for your bodily health; I had recurring visits with Jesus in the Blessed Sacrament for soul and spiritual health. I was in such a hurry that I hadn't even warmed up my car. My father was standing outside too and I couldn't wait to get away from him. He had been getting on my nerves for a couple of days prior. I was also overtired. I was jobless too. (Being unemployed meant I was home too much and it was a contributing factor to low self-esteem.) I stayed at the chapel for two hours and felt better when I got home.

God restored the peer relationships I lost during my teenage years. He sent me a friend I met at one of my old part-time jobs, Paula, to show me what a healthy, normal, female-to-female relationship should be. I had no sexual attraction to her whatsoever. It was purely friendship. That is what I was lacking all those years. Lonnie explained that I was going through the psycho-sexual stage all over again—like an adolescent. I was like a thirteen year old reliving what I missed out on, what I was supposed to have beginning at that age and continuing throughout my teenage years. God is a restorer; He will restore all your lost years. "And I will restore to you the years that the locust has eaten…" (Joel 2:25). And, when you seek Him with all of your heart and delight yourself in Him, He will give you the desires of your heart. He will give you what you want or need. "Delight yourself in the LORD; And He will give you the desires of your heart" (Psalms 37:4).

I also connected with some college friends that summer (one male, too: Keith—strictly platonic). We all went out together dancing, doing day trips and overnight excursions to the shore. In every place we stayed, I put a picture of Jesus on the dresser. Paula even made a comment one time to Keith (she had a crush on him) that I was "too religious." He didn't think anything was wrong with that! I went with another friend from college to Puerto Rico. What made these experiences unique was that everything was happening so fast in such a short period of time. And, the funny part was, I wasn't working at the time. I don't know how I was able to do all these things without any income. I know now that it was God. He was providing all of it for me. "And my God shall supply all your needs according to His riches in glory in Christ Jesus" (Philippians 4:19). And, if you put God first and seek and go after Him with all your heart (what I did), He will deliver. "But seek first the Kingdom of God and his righteousness, and all these things will be given to you as well" (Matthew 6:33).

Let's not forget, too, that "He is a rewarder of those that diligently seek him" (Hebrews 11:6). Again I have to say, this is truly amazing. Even more amazing was that in a little over a year from the time I gave my life to Jesus Christ, I was standing in front of the group of Encourage members, giving my testimony.

6.
WITHSTANDING THE STORMS

The storms of life, or in this case, temptations, are always going to come. We just need to make sure we don't entertain them or allow them to dominate our lives. "And he said to his disciples, 'Temptations to sin are sure to come…'" (Luke 17:1). Again, the woman from Encourage spoke to me. She told me not to be discouraged; temptations are a part of life. She referred to individuals who were struggling with weight. She said it's like putting a hot fudge sundae directly in front of one of those people. It is only natural! I believe that's the first, basic step to not giving in to temptation—to avoid it in the first place. Stay away from those areas, people, or places that may lead you into sin.

The first step for me was breaking away from all my gay friends and avoiding the gay bars and nightclubs. The second step was taking down all the posters of women and reminders in my room. The third step was avoiding watching sexual scenes on television and in movies. And then there was music. Music was hard for me because I liked so many songs. But, I thought of God when I listened to the lyrics instead of allowing my mind to drift off towards a woman. For example, in the song, "Total Eclipse of the Heart" by Nicki French (1994 dance remake of Bonnie Tyler's 1983 version), one of the lyrics states, "Turn around—every now and then I know there's no one in the universe as magical and wondrous as you." God was (and still is) that person! In her 1997 dance song, "This Is Your Night," Amber sings, "So in love with you, Oh yeah, it's too good to be true!" I thought about being in love with God. Gala's 1997 hit song, "Freed from Desire," was my theme.

I can't overestimate the power of the mind when it comes to dealing with temptation and being dead to sins. "So you also must consider yourselves dead to sin and alive to God in Christ Jesus" (Romans 6:11). It all starts in the mind. It is where Satan tries to manipulate you. When I feel a lustful thought arise when I see an attractive woman, I say, "I'm dead to that sin." If it is dead in your mind, if you do not think it or play it out like a movie in your mind, it will not manifest in your life. Your thoughts lead to beliefs which lead to actions. They all go hand in hand. "For as he thinks within himself, so he is" (Proverbs 23:7).

I believe this also ties in with sin breeding sin. Being envious leads to fantasizing evil thoughts, fantasizing evil thoughts leads to acting out, acting out leads to lying, lying leads to moving away from family and from God. This can lead to drunkenness, which leads to lustful thoughts, which leads to fornication and/or masturbation, and so on and so forth. I realized some of this was happening in my own life. Homosexual desire really became "dead" to me when I stopped thinking about it and entertaining it. Here, the phrase, "Out of sight, out of mind," applies too. (Remember what I mentioned earlier about being aware of what you watch in movies and on television. And, even in real life!) As Joyce Meyer said, you have to stop feeding the flesh. If you stop feeding it, it will eventually die. It will be hard at first and your flesh will be screaming, but the more you stop feeding it, the easier it will become. You might think a past relationship or situation in your life is over, but if it is alive in your mind, it is

6. Withstanding the Storms

indeed alive in your life. You will never be free from it until it is dead to you.

You have to "see" yourself as a beautiful, feminine woman of God. Since I modeled myself after my father, in my mind's eye I was or wanted to be a man—even though I looked beautifully female on the outside. You would never know it! I believe the truth, in accordance with Ephesians 1:4 and Psalm 139 as I quoted earlier. God created each of us distinctly male and female. He knew when we would come into existence before the world began and gave each of us a planned purpose and assignment. You were created as a man or woman for a divine purpose! Thanks to Joyce, I also say, "God thinks I'm amazing. God thinks I'm wonderful." It is very healing to recite those things to yourself.

Even today, I am slowly perceiving myself as a woman. A short time ago at the beauty salon, I realized this. My hairdresser is the epitome of femininity. She is also very sweet and kind. My family and I often refer to her as a china doll. If I let myself, when she is cutting my hair, I could easily fall into temptation. Now what good would that do? (I love the way she cuts, so I wouldn't think of going somewhere else. Plus, it's near my house and we've been going there for years.) As she was working, even before any temptation set in, I said to myself, "She is my equal, not my idol." It worked! I just made it up right there, by the grace of God. I began to see myself as "level" with her. I tried to see that I was just like her, sweet and beautiful too (like I mentioned earlier with Tina Fey). Instead of putting beautiful women up on a pedestal like they're a different part of my world, I have to see that I am just like them, and that they are just like me. They *are* part of my world. By seeing myself as equal with them, that we are the same, the attraction subsides. This makes sense of course, because opposites attract.

The best way to combat temptation is with the Word of God. Remember, we are constantly fighting a spiritual battle. The sword of the spirit is the best defense. "Take the helmet of salvation and the sword of the Spirit, which is the word of God" (Ephesians 6:17). When I started to doubt or became unsure about my decision to follow God, I used Jesus' words at Calvary: "Father, if you are willing, take this cup away from me. Yet not my will but yours be done" (Luke 22:42). Asking Jesus to cleanse me with His precious blood worked wonderfully.

Waking up is another difficult, tempting time—when you're in your alpha state. Satan tries to get everybody who is grappling in one way or another or weak in any area, in the morning. It's probably because our defenses our down and Satan uses that to his advantage. It is the perfect time for him to influence our thoughts. He also wants to start us off and set us up for a disastrous day. It is very important to be cognizant of this, not only so you know how to strike back, but so you know that it is normal—so that you don't beat yourself up over it.

I still struggle in this area. Just recently I was watching television and started having tempting thoughts about an actress I admired. I don't remember exactly what happened, but I know it was heading in the wrong direction. In my semi-conscious state, I said to myself (yes, not even out loud), *Satan, get thee away from me*. This is in the Bible where Jesus turned to Peter and said, "Get thee behind me, Satan..." (Matthew 16:23). Then, the thoughts just seemed to vanish from my mind. It was like they were pushed down or aside. It was astonishing.

A priest once said in a sermon at a local church that Jesus gave us words to use and not to be afraid to use them. Especially the words He used when tempted by the devil. Jesus answered, "It is written: 'Man shall not live on bread alone, but on every word that comes from the mouth of God'" (Matthew 4:4). The bread relates to our fleshly desires, and we do not need to live or act out on them. It is the Word of God that we need to act on.

Another scripture that I learned about is Galatians 5:16: "But I say, walk by the Spirit, and you will not gratify the desires of the flesh." This was and is another approach that worked for me when I saw an attractive woman and felt some lust creeping up. I recited it just once, and again, the feeling subsided. One time I saw a man giving a testimony on television on how he got over lustful thoughts towards women and that was the exact quote he used. He meditated on it for about two weeks, and he began to see women's bodies in a godly way—as pure, beautiful works of art from their Creator, God. So, instead of looking at the anatomy of a woman in a sinful way, we must strive to see it as God does.

Not long ago, I watched famous preacher Dr. Charles Stanley's message on temptation. He said to stop it before it enters your mind, and visualize yourself doing the right thing. He also said to say to yourself, *It could destroy my life. This is not who I am.* Then look at the big picture. Furthermore, I came across what Dr. David Jeremiah said. It was something to the effect of focusing on what God, or your Master, would want you to do. He said to think of God watching over us and looking down on us, just as a human owner watches over and looks down on his dog. When a dog almost does something he should not do, he looks up at his master or owner. Because he loves and admires his master, he does not do it. Just like that dog, we must gaze up at our master or owner, almighty God, and know He is guarding us. Because of that special bond and mutual love, we are deterred from doing the wrong thing.

It's important to know that another cause of temptation is not having certain needs met. Maybe you have a need to feel good about yourself or a need for high self-esteem. You may also have a need for acceptance. I noticed that when I felt good about myself, I felt less temptation. For example, I never got tempted at the gym because when I was working out, I felt good about myself. Exercise is good for everything. It is a mood lifter as it releases endorphins, the feel good chemical, from your brain. It helps me when I am faced with all kinds of difficult situations.

In May 1996, we had a party for my nephew's first Communion. I remember feeling good in my red dress, greeting and guiding the guests as they walked in. I was confident and held myself in high regard. I wasn't tempted at all that day.

That same month, I had the honor of being a bridesmaid (my first) for my friend Marcietta's wedding. She had asked me at the perfect time—God's perfect timing. I received the phone call when I was having a bad night. I was down and out, lonely, perhaps I was being tempted. After we finished speaking, I felt a world of difference. For me, this is a manifestation of Corinthians 10:13, which bears repeating: "But God is faithful, who will not suffer you to be tempted above that ye are able; but with the temptation also make a way to escape, that ye may be able to bear it."

The entire preparation and anticipation of the event was enjoyable. On the actual wedding day, I started out with a great make-up application from a local beauty salon. Another bridesmaid and friend of the family, Fanny, told me my eyes looked like almonds as they were so accentuated. My hair was in great shape too. The dresses were a salmon color, the color that brings out the best in me. Needless to say, I was feeling very good about myself. I was the belle of the ball! Instead of it being the bride's day, Fanny said it was my day.

I had a great time with the girls in the limousine. We talked, laughed, and drank champagne, all in good fun. I felt accepted. I felt as one with them. As gorgeous as they all were, again, I was not tempted at all that day.

Another time on our way home from a great time at a night club, I was strolling down the block with two other girlfriends I had some feelings for in the past, myself in the middle. We were walking arm-in-arm, frolicking. Again, I felt as one with them. I was accepted. I wasn't tempted at all.

Additionally, you should know that temptation strikes most when you are hungry, angry, lonely, or tired. When you are experiencing these, of course, there are other needs involved that are not being met. That Encourage member I keep referring back to (God bless her!) once referred to these as H.A.L.T. How appropriate! When you are feeling hungry (H), angry (A), lonely (L), or tired (T), you have to be even more aware that temptation might hit. And when it does, you say out loud, "HALT!" And it works. It helps to know why you feel the temptation, and it is very satisfying to know that there is a reason for it. Then, you're able to recognize it as something false. You don't give credence to the tempting thoughts. I think I've had all of these at one time or another. Lonnie helped me recognize when I was in one of these situations.

Although I don't recall ever being tempted while hungry, it makes sense that when this basic, physiological need is not met, your mind can't function in the proper way. (And, speaking of physiological, I noticed that I was more tempted two weeks after I menstruated, during ovulation.) No wonder why when people are hungry, sometimes they say, "I can't think straight!" And, you do become more emotional when you are hungry. I know I can easily lose my temper or become angry when I don't eat for a long period of time.

Anger, of course, as discussed earlier, is a big contributing factor to temptation. (Remember, when I was mad at my father, I was so tempted to give up.) It could also be that when we're angry, we become careless about doing what's right and just want what we want, again, without thinking straight. We might think we are entitled to it—and we would be acting on emotion. Have you ever heard a person who is on a diet become angry and say, "I'm so mad at her! I don't care! I'm going to eat that cake even if it kills me!"? I certainly have.

If we behave angrily or act on anger, it is sinful, and sin breeds sin. If you are feeling lonely, you are probably in need of acceptance or self-esteem. When this happens, pick up the phone and call a friend or the person who holds you accountable.

It works almost every time. If there are certain times or nights when you know loneliness is going to strike, make plans ahead of time to spend time with family or friends.

When we're tired, our emotions are all messed up. We are always more emotional when we're tired. When we dream during a peaceful, restful sleep, or during the delta stage, we release underlying emotions. Thus, it is an "emotional release." If we don't get to do this while sleeping, we will be more emotional during our wakeful state. Sleep affects the amygdala, the emotional part of the brain. When it is well rested, it is much less sensitive. In other words, a sleep-deprived amygdala will go awry. We will react much more emotionally in response to fear, anxiety, etc. It is no wonder why we would be much more emotional with our feelings too! If I was sleep deprived for just one night, I would feel lust coming over me just by looking at a friend's leg while she was driving! (I did have feelings for this girl though—Alana. But more on that later.) Thankfully, I knew that I was just overtired. I ignored it, and it quickly went away.

For the same reasons as waking, drifting off to sleep is a major tempting time. Your guard is down. You must focus on Jesus and prayers here. One night, I was watching my Christian television in bed and relaxing before I went to sleep, just as I was in the last stages of writing this book. This buxom woman I liked was on, speaking. Soon I felt my thoughts start to drift to lying on her bosom. Where did this come from? Well, it was dark, and maybe it happened because I was close to agreeing to a contract to publish this book and Satan tried to discourage me. Or maybe God wanted me to include it here to help you, and who knows? Temptation can strike at any time. Anyway, before the thought had any time to grow, I said to myself, *I don't need that anymore. No! I have Jesus now. He meets all my needs abundantly.* Guess what? It worked! I felt more spiritual and peaceful, and the desire diminished.

6. Withstanding the Storms

Other temptation triggers are the holidays and the change of seasons. Holidays always play with our emotions, especially if we spend them alone or have lost a loved one. Seasonal change, or the transition between winter and spring, spring and summer, summer and fall, and fall and winter, can dramatically affect our emotional state. The temperature shift probably conjures up certain feelings or moods. (A cloudy day can drastically affect my mood!) I have experienced temptation during these times myself. Since I knew where it was coming from, it didn't bother me. I simply accepted it and didn't give it a second thought.

There's a certain tactic I used called "attention refocused" at times when I wanted to think about a woman. Instead of focusing my attention on a woman, I would turn my attention toward good, healthy thoughts about a man. And, I quickly diverted my mind to loving thoughts toward that guy Mickey I met at that night club in the city. I pictured myself enjoying his company. It could be any man that had physical potential for me—a man I thought I once liked, an actor, or even a fictional character or someone I made up in my mind. For example, when I was out dancing one night with the girls at a local night club, I started to notice the women around me on the dancefloor. As soon as I became aware of it, I quickly diverted my mind towards Mickey. I pictured him dancing with me.

When I was tempted to fantasize, especially while falling asleep at night or waking up in the morning, I could refocus my mind on healthy thoughts about a man or picture myself as a beautiful woman in the mirror of my mind. Sometimes I did not want to divert my mind, but I did it anyway. Like I learned from Joyce, your feelings will catch up with your thoughts, little by little. Eventually, when I put this into practice, I actually felt something at the thought of Mickey. How exciting! There was a slight change in my heart rate. It was higher. Could it be? Yes, it did happen at the time. Of course, there's much more to healing than that, but I think it was a great start!

Last but certainly not least, I learned that just because something feels right and normal to you, doesn't mean it is right and normal. It took me a while to accept this. I used to say, *How could something be so wrong when it feels so right?* A line in Whitney Houston's song, "How Will I Know," is, "Don't trust your feelings." We can't base or live our lives on emotion or feelings but on what the Word of God says. Dr. Stanley preached on living a life based on principle instead of preference. And, as Joyce says, we must align our thoughts with God's thoughts and, as I just mentioned, our feelings will follow. We have to get in agreement with the Bible, believe the truth of the Bible, and the right feelings will come. It will take time, but it is most certainly worth it. Just think what the world would be like if everyone just lived according to what they were feeling. There would be more murder, incest, bestiality, etc. And they would *all* be okay. I now think of homosexuality as that of pedophilia. It feels so natural to that person, but morally and absolutely, it is not natural.

I know this is easier said than done. I am only human too. We live in a fallen world. Just because I acquired all this knowledge and truth through the grace of God doesn't mean I haven't had any major bumps along the way. Just when you think you have it all together, unexpected circumstances arise that could throw you off course. "Therefore, in order to keep me from becoming conceited, I was given a thorn in my flesh, a messenger of Satan…" (2 Corinthians 12:7).

7.

BLOWS ALONG MY BARK

I was pretty much flying high between 1996 and 1998. I just started a new job with a publishing company in the city, still went out and traveled with friends, and I began graduate school. I was still somewhat tempted by friends, but I considered it "normal" under the circumstances and didn't make any major issues out of it.

In early 1999, I shared a short testimony in the city with Courage that they were going to air on EWTN's, *The World Over*, with Raymond Arroyo. The weekend after I did that, I felt God had rewarded me. I had an avid prayer life and continued to attend daily mass and frequent the Perpetual Adoration Chapel. Then, just when I thought it was all over, a massive blow burst my bubble.

At some point in the middle of the year (1999), I developed a serious crush on my supervisor, Alana. It was very hard not to, as she was patient, sweet, kind, and always made me feel like I was the most important person in the world. She was always concerned that I was not being challenged enough. I remember when I had a bout with bronchitis and I didn't want to be out of the office for too long. It was going on close to two weeks. When I told her, she said to me, "Don't worry about that. We just care about your health." What boss would say *that*? She was well liked by everyone. She always gave people the benefit of the doubt. It was very easy to see how one could fall for her. She was a few years older than I was, petite, with brown hair and brown eyes—similar to me (remember what I said earlier about Tina Fey). We quickly clicked and became friends. We went out to lunch together, went shopping, and talked in her office for long periods for time. She was *never* too busy. I kept track of what time she left at the end of the day so I could ride the elevator with her. I so looked forward to going to work all the time!

Soon after we all got laid off, Alana and I lost touch for a couple of years. When I learned her husband had passed away in 2003, I contacted her. I was so thrilled the first time I went to her house. Consequently, we started spending more time together and became closer. Since we were both unemployed and coping with emotional issues, we found much needed support and encouragement from one another. I saw qualities in her that I didn't recognize in myself (one of the causes of SSA, as I mentioned earlier), primarily strength, courageousness, and her laid-back style. I could foresee myself falling into a dependent relationship with her.

To prevent this from happening, I made sure that I spent equal time with my other friends and tried not to see her on a weekly basis. I recognized and accepted this as the "thorn in my flesh." Nevertheless, since she lived alone with her two small daughters, I often shared dinner with her and slept over at her house (later on, I shared her bed with her). Her eldest called me "Auntie JM." She always made me feel so comfortable and welcome. We went out all the time—dinner, clubbing, plays—as long as she could get a babysitter. She picked me up and drove me home. In retrospect, it was like dating without the physical aspect.

7. Blows Along My Bark

We travelled too: overnight trips, short trips, long trips. When I was with Alana, I had not a care in the world. We were having a ball. When I dropped her off after a one or two night trip, I felt horrible. I was so emotional. It was more than sadness. I felt as if something was ripped away from me. It was like a great loss, a major emptiness. It is hard to explain. It was like I couldn't go on without her. That's how the relationship is (as I spoke about earlier). It is *very* unhealthy.

Friendly massages were the extent of our physical contact. It was strictly platonic; she was one hundred percent attracted to men. (I thank God now that she was!) I never told Alana how I felt about her; her friendship was too important to me to risk losing. She was very intelligent—she probably knew all along! She considered me the sister she never had. In the meantime, I fell hard for her. I would do anything for her. I wanted to do everything and anything with her. I idolized her. I was very protective of her and the girls. I started to take the role of the male. That was not good! Of course, I knew to have that kind of relationship with her was wrong, but my feelings for her were so strong and seemed so real. This is a classic example of how you should not trust your feelings.

My downfall (or blessing in disguise) came one evening in 2005 while we were dancing at a local night club. A guy, Benny, approached us not long after we started dancing. He was attracted to Alana. He later left the dancefloor but accosted us again later at the bar while we were engrossed in a conversation. I was growing more and more agitated. Alana, being polite as she is, started talking to him. Much to my chagrin, he remained with us for the rest of the night. She ended up giving him her phone number. Needless to say, I was very distraught over this and I couldn't stop thinking about it. I knew I was letting the situation take control of me and I had to stop it; I had to let it go.

I had a picture of the two of us in my bedroom on my nightstand. It was at a restaurant from 2004, when we first really started to go out on a regular basis. I knew I had to distance myself from her a little, so I removed it. It was the last thing I saw before I closed my eyes at night and the first thing I saw when I woke up in the morning. I used to say "goodnight" to it (her) amongst other affectionate things. I also used to make loving gestures towards it. I knew this was very unhealthy, especially since the more you outwardly verbalize or perform an action, the more it becomes believable and real to you. So, I confidently placed it on the other side of the room where it was much less visible.

One time when I still felt feelings for her arise after I settled into bed at night, I said wholeheartedly, "Jesus, please take these feelings away from me." And in an instant, He did. The next thing I did was start saying the rosary and Chaplet of Divine mercy again, daily, as I had stopped committing myself to them over the past few years. Within a few weeks, I noticed that my relationship with her began to improve. I no longer idolized her as much; I approached her more as my equal. Yet, I still faced the struggle almost daily. Thoughts I shouldn't be having continued to pop into my head, and I had to constantly stop them before they turned into fantasies. I outwardly said, "Stop it, (JM), Stop it!" Then I focused my thoughts on something else. H.A.L.T. holds true. I was often hungry, angry, lonely (bored), or tired when the thoughts taunted me the most. Sometimes I'd just remind myself that she was no better than I was. But the most important thing to do is spend time with Jesus in the Blessed Sacrament, which I had to make an effort to do more often.

I thought things were going pretty well with my relationship with her until a few weeks later when I called her one night and she wasn't home. When I messaged her during the day to ask her if she would be home and she didn't reply, it made the situation even worse. Immediately, the notion that she might be out with Benny from the night club flashed into my mind and I went into a frenzy. Just the thought of it made me nauseous. I ranted

7. Blows Along My Bark

and raved for a few hours, analyzing and venting. My family and friends were there to support me, but I still felt like I was on the brink of insanity. I knew it was crazy to be feeling this way! She had every right to go out with whomever she wanted, whenever she wanted. She wasn't doing me any injustice. I was building the whole thing up in my mind. I knew the only person that was going to get me out of this mess was Jesus. So by the time midnight came, I turned on the prayer channel and took out all my prayers and scripture quotes that I had tucked away a few years ago. I also read Psalm 139 and a letter from God the Father I used to read, telling all about His love for me. I would like to share it with you:

Dearest:

I love you and my love for you is eternal. Do not look at your limitations, but look to me, I am eternal. Do not look at your weakness, but look to me, I am Almighty. Do not look at your sin, but trust in my mercy.

I love you now, this moment. You are precious to me, you are worthy of esteem, and I love you. For you are the masterpiece of Creation. You are my joy. Even if the mountains would move, my affection for you would not cease.

I have always been at your side, even when you didn't notice, even when you didn't feel my presence. I was there to support you, to enlighten you. I have been with you wherever you have gone. Even when you rejected me, I was there to love you.

I love you. Of this you must be certain! Nothing and no one should ever let you doubt this. I love you! Whenever you sin, do not doubt my mercy, for I love you. Whenever you are alone, I want you to know that I am on your side. I will never leave or abandon you.

If you should have to pass through a river, I will be with you, you will not drown. If you should have to walk through fire, the flames will not harm you; you will not be burned.

I have an assignment for you. Many of my children are desperate because they do not know me. They do not know I love them and that my love for them is deep. For this reason I say to you: go amongst my people, meet as many as you can and tell each of them, "<u>God Loves YOU</u> now, this very moment."

Tell them I am at their side and I will never forget them. I am counting on you. Remember if you do not tell them, many of them will despair. Tell them about my immense love; tell them about my tenderness, about my forgiveness.

I AM COUNTING ON YOU!

Signed,

GOD, YOUR FATHER

I cried and prayed and held on to an 8 × 10 picture of the Sacred Heart for an hour. I finally felt peaceful and more accepting of the situation. I rested and fell asleep, assured of God's love for me.

It turned out that Alana wasn't out with Benny after all. I just had to come to the realization that if she ever did or when she decided to go out with anybody else it would not affect her relationship with me. As hard as it was, I was prepared with the sword of the Spirit. And with the help of Jesus, I would be happy for her. I prayed daily for a healthy friendship, as I wanted to continue to play out my role in her life—as "the sister she never had." Knowing and saying this is one thing, but, of course, acting on it is another. It surely is a process! Alana saw Benny

7. BLOWS ALONG MY BARK

maybe once or twice after that, but she realized he was no good for her. He still called her occasionally, and I would feel my anger and jealously flaring up when he did! But eventually, he stopped.

Alana and I continued to have fun, memorable times together. Then, a major shift occurred in our relationship in November 2008. The inevitable happened. She started seeing this guy, John, one of her friend's husband's friends. After they all went out for a casual dinner one evening, he started sending her flowers, calling her every night, and buying her lots of nice things. To my surprise, I handled it well. (Although I didn't like the fact that October 2008 was the last time we saw each other on a Saturday night.)

Things progressed quickly with Alana and John. He often called her when I was at her house; I patiently waited for her to get off the phone so I could have my time with her. Believe it or not, I liked John when I first met him. He was very intelligent and well to do. He also got along well with her daughters. By the grace of God, I accepted the situation. March 2009 was Alana and my last trip together.

During that time, I reconnected with an old college friend, Gail, through social media. Gail and I began to socialize together. Not long after, she broke up with her boyfriend after eighteen years, which allowed us to spend even more time together. We went to dinner, night clubs, and on all kinds of trips—similar things I did with Alana. This time, it was mutually platonic. Gail kept me so busy that I didn't have time to think about Alana and John. This is a prime example of God's providence. Just as God brought John into Alana's life, and her time for me waned, God, in His perfect timing, gave me Gail. God knew I needed that. Philippians 4:19 says, "And my God shall supply all your needs." Who knows how I would have handled the loss if I didn't have Gail. God knew! And He knew I needed a friend.

First Corinthians 10:13 says that He will provide a way of escape. Turns out, He provided me as a way of escape for Gail, too, as she was devastated after she broke up with her boyfriend. (A few years later, in 2011, she met someone else, at a time when I didn't need her as much—at the same exact time Alana and John moved out of the city.) Moreover, I believe God sent me to Alana to help her cope after the devastating loss of her husband. Why God sent Alana into my life, I am still pondering. Maybe it was the "thorn in my flesh," or maybe I was not completely healed. Maybe my needs were still not being met? Remember, again, it is a process. Maybe God allowed it to happen so I could use it to help others. As televangelist Dr. Mike Murdoch said, God creates everything and everyone for a solution to a problem. For example, we have glasses to solve the problem of seeing; we have mugs to solve the problem of drinking; etc. We are each individually created to solve a problem. Whether it is a societal problem or the solution to someone else's problem, we should know, be constantly aware, and live according to this awesome fact.

Alana and I are still very good friends, but nothing like we used to be. We see each other only a couple of times a year. No more steady trips. No more physical contact. God took her away from me as much as He needed, but not completely. He distanced her as much as I could sustain a normal, healthy friendship with her. It had to happen. How long could I go on with her that way? It was not good for me. I probably would not have written this book. Plus, I had served my purpose in her life. The season was over. "For everything there is a season, and a time for every purpose under heaven" (Ecclesiastes 3:1). Now, by the grace of God, the bondage is broken. The feelings ceased. What a liberating feeling it is, not to be a slave to your passions and emotions. How great it is, not to have her drop me off or have her leave without getting clingy and teary-eyed. No more unhealthy emotional attachment. I even slept over at her and John's apartment knowing they were in the same bed without it bothering me! That was a major breakthrough for me.

7. Blows Along My Bark

Another reason for this freedom was that I stopped it in my mind. I stopped thinking about Alana in that way. And again, out of sight, out of mind. Remember what I said earlier, that if it is alive in your mind, it is alive in your life.

The reason I am telling you this story is because I thought I would *never* get over her. If I can do it, so can you. If God did it for me, He can do it for you. Never say never. You are capable of more than you know. And most importantly, "Nothing is impossible with God" (Luke 1:37).

In 1999, the same time I was working with Alana, I was introduced to a Russian woman, Viktoria, through a college friend. Viktoria was fun and down-to-earth, so we hit it off right away. We went out dancing with friends all the time. I often picked her up and drove her home because she lived close by. As time went on, I found out Viktoria considered herself bisexual. This revelation didn't affect me much because I had absolutely no attraction to her whatsoever. Nonetheless, as we went out dancing on a regular basis, she made passes at me. Unfortunately, one night, I got caught up in the heat of the moment.

This is a perfect example of putting yourself in a tempting position. These situations should be avoided at all costs. It was bound to happen. With a drink or two in me, and as we were engrossed in the music and the atmosphere of the night club, I succumbed. This is "sin breeding sin." What St. Paul says in Romans 7:18-20 about struggling with sin also comes to mind: "I know that nothing good lives in me, that is, in my flesh; for I have the desire to do what is good, but I cannot carry it out. For I do not do the good I want to do. Instead, I keep on doing the evil I do not want to do. And if I do what I do not want, it is no longer I who do it, but it is sin living in me that does it." Here St. Paul describes the double life we lead: the flesh (the sinful human nature), and the spirit (Christ dwelling within).

I'm not going to get into the details, but over the next four years, I furtively engaged in behaviors I am not proud of. (And, yes, we did go to gay clubs sometimes.) Of course, I knew it was wrong. We never did go "all the way," but I still wonder if those incidents were obstacles to my complete healing. Why did this happen? As I mentioned earlier, we are still human and live in a fallen world. I was frequenting environments that encouraged sin, but since I loved music and dancing so much, I often overlooked that aspect of them. Was I still weak? Maybe God allowed me to experience this to make me even stronger in the long run. Maybe this was another "thorn in my flesh."

We will not know the answers to everything here on earth. God likes mysteries. If He reveals everything to us and life always runs smoothly, we would no longer need to depend on Him. I want to make clear that I felt nowhere to Viktoria how I felt about Alana. This was solely fleshly lust. I did not want a relationship or to partake of that lifestyle with Viktoria whatsoever. That's the main thing. Even though I experienced these feelings, I never swayed from the truth. But, we are all going to fall, just like Jesus did. "Though he fall, he shall not be utterly cast down: for the LORD upholds him with his hand" (Psalm 37:24).

The most important thing is that we get up and try again. There will always be bumps along the road. Remember, as I quote from Joyce Meyer, "You do not have to win every battle to win the war." Maybe this happened because it was meant, like Alana's, to be added to my life story to help you. As I continue to ponder, it may be a combination of all these things. Today, Viktoria and I maintain a normal, healthy friendship. The moral is I got through it, and it did end, although, like my season with Alana, I thought it *never* would. Don't ever give in or give up! "Let us not grow weary in well doing, for in due time we will reap a harvest, if we do not give up" (Galatians 6:9).

8.

BASKING IN THE WARMTH OF GOD'S RAYS

Today, I trust and rest in God and continue to lead an active prayer life. "Instead he disciplined them so they would trust in God alone" (Deuteronomy 8). I still pray for true femininity and heterosexuality, although I learned recently that instead of praying for heterosexuality we should be praying for wholeness. I often declare: *By Your stripes and precious shed blood I am healed.* I thank God for creating me a woman and making me His daughter, and sometimes I recite affirmations such as, *I am a beautiful woman of God; I clearly identify myself with the woman God created me to be; God is my Father; I can love, trust, and be intimate with a man;* and *men are GOOD.* I pray to keep learning the truth about men, sexuality, and marriage. I pray that God continues to prepare that special male for me, and me for him, if it is His will. If He doesn't, I pray for the grace to be happy anyway and not to lose my joy. I pray that God allows it to happen only if it doesn't interfere with His will for my life or my assignment. I pray that God keeps my eyes and ears open to the Holy Spirit and helps me not to be deceived. I go on to thank God for saving me from a life of destruction and abomination. I thank Him for showing me the truth. To this day when I hear the song "Amazing Grace" sung at my church, it brings tears to my eyes. "Here I Am Lord" also touches me and gives me strength every time I hear it.

On my not so good days, in Joyce Meyer's words, I say, "I may not be where I want to be, but thank God I am not where I *used* to be. I'm okay and I'm on my way!" Also, thanks to her, when things seem to be moving along more slowly than I would like, I say, "God is working in my life right now," and, "My times are in His hands." God is working in the spiritual realm behind the scenes in our lives. He is making a way and rearranging circumstances so everything works for His glory, in His perfect timing. Although we may not see or feel it, He is. There are still times when I ask, *Why did this have to happen to me?* And there are times when I feel a twinge of jealously toward heterosexual couples. But, if all of this hadn't happened to me, I would not have this close relationship with God that I have now, and I would not have been exposed to all this truth. I probably would have forever thought I was supposed to be a boy, stuck inside a woman's body. (Yes, I did feel that way at one time.) I might have physically changed my gender! I probably still would be living in fear of evolution and the ascent of man.

I once heard Joyce state, "What Satan intends for evil God uses for good." I know that He will bring something wonderful out of it (remember Romans 8:28), such as this book to (hopefully) save many. "I am the vine; you are the branches. If you remain in me and I in you, you will bear much fruit; apart from me you can do nothing" (John 15:5). And, He has used my circumstances to fulfill my dream of becoming a real, published author. Your history doesn't have to become your destiny. As Joyce (again!) says, your test will become your testimony and your mess will become your message.

8. Basking in the Warmth of God's Rays

I have to admit that it has not been easy. In no way do I want to discourage you, I am just being honest. But, as we all know, nothing good comes easy. Hard is good. Remember, "Those who sow in tears will reap in joy" (Psalm 126:5). And, "For whatever a man sows, this he will also reap" (Galatians 6:7). It has certainly been a long process and journey, and it continues. God is not finished with me yet! I recently learned from Joyce that He works by the law of gradual growth. She explained that we see this in nature in plants. If we stared at a plant or flower for several days, we would think, *this is not growing*. It would look exactly the same. But over a long period of time, we would see the major shift to a full, mature product of nature, a complete work and manifestation of the glory of God. She also says that we change in stages. Our transformation is like that of a caterpillar's metamorphosis; it happens in distinct stages. This is exactly how God works in us. It makes sense, if you think about it. If we changed drastically overnight, it would be a psychological shock to our being! As long as we keep doing the right thing, He changes us from glory to glory. "But we all…are being transformed into the same image from glory to glory" (2 Corinthians 3:18).

As I mentioned earlier, I am still well aware of the movies and television shows I watch and books that I read (no sexually explicit scenes, and mostly Christian). I try to avoid temptation at all costs. (And, my clubbing days are over!) Even so, like Joyce says, I'd rather go all the way with God than be stuck living a life of a lie all by myself. I can't wait to see what God has in store for me. "For God alone my soul waits" (Psalm 62:1).

Two scriptures that I meditate on often in this area that give me hope are, "The One having begun a good work in you will complete it until the day of Christ Jesus" (Philippians 1:6), and, "Now to Him who is able to do far more abundantly beyond all that we ask or think, according to the power that works within us" (Ephesians 3:20). Later on, I added another scripture: "No good thing does He withhold from those who walk uprightly" (Psalm 84:11). And as preacher Joel Osteen continues, "And that good thing is going to be manifest according to His perfect will and timing." I also remember Joel referring to Psalm 84:6, saying that in passing through the valley of weeping, you will find pools of blessing. Stay in faith, knowing God has something better. He will take those tears and turn them into pools to refresh you. Joel also refers to God as the God of the "suddenlys." God can make anything happen at any time. Suddenly, you can have your breakthrough. You never know! Don't forget, "Weeping may endure for a night, but joy comes in the morning" (Psalm 30:5). Besides, our time here on earth is phenomenally short compared with eternity. We will get all our answers, reap rewards, and find our true pleasure in heaven.

Keep in mind that you are on the potter's wheel. God is molding you, forming your character, making you stronger, and maturing you. Remember James 1:2-4: "Consider it pure joy, my brothers, when you face trials of many kinds, because you know that the testing of your faith develops perseverance. Perseverance must finish its work so that you may be mature and complete, not lacking anything." It is good to go through tough times. They stretch us and change us into the women God created us to be. They prepare us for harder times ahead. I learned from Joyce that there is treasure is trials. And every time you do the right thing when you feel like doing the wrong thing, you are growing. God loves us too much to leave us alone. As I learned with Lonnie twenty-two years ago from a testimonial, "God loves us but loves us too much to leave us there." We have to step out of our comfort zone. It is like wearing an old shoe. It's all we know, and we can get so used to it, we don't know it will hurt us in the long run. Like a new shoe, the new life God has in store for us will be uncomfortable at first, but once we step into it, we'll never want to go back to the old one.

8. Basking in the Warmth of God's Rays

We are all human and live in a fallen world, stained from original sin. I still face temptation every now and then. When I do, I clearly know where it comes from and it is totally manageable. It doesn't rule over me anymore. I am no longer a slave to my passions. As long as we live on this earth, we may never be 100 percent free of feelings of temptation. I read in a Regeneration newsletter dated February 2002 that we (men, but who is to say this can't be true for women too), "get programmed in such a way that things that used to cause a sexual response in us long ago still have the capacity to bring up that response. It's like a circuit has been burned in our brains, and it never fully goes away. Our responses may be purely physical. It is not a sign of what we really want now, nor does it mean that we still have some deep unmet needs that are about to surface again. After a few weeks, we may rarely think of the episode."

Once in a while I will have a tempting dream that will leave me unnerved. A few minutes after waking, the feeling is *totally* gone. I would think, *Why would I be having these dreams if I don't feel this way when I'm fully awake?* Perhaps it has to do with that circuit in our brains; there is so much we don't know about our unconscious minds. Or, maybe it is Satan's way of attacking since he can't get to me consciously. Like I mentioned earlier, we'll find the answers someday. The most important thing is that I never want to go back into that lifestyle. I want to live by the truth and live a life pleasing to God and not the devil. Once God has gotten His eternal grip on you, you will want this too. It is unbelievable to think at one time, eons ago, I longed for a woman. I desired to be in a woman's arms so much that I used to write heart wrenching poems about it. The mere fact that this longing has disappeared is nothing short of a miracle that can only be explained by divine intervention.

Last but certainly not least, I want God to proud of me. Don't you want Him to be proud of you too? There is an inner peace I have knowing I am doing God's will and knowing the truth

He has revealed to me. He enlightened me with a knowledge and understanding that most people don't possess. He obliterated my crippling terror of evolution. In short, He transformed my life. And He will do the same for you.

> *David also said to Solomon his son, "Be strong and courageous, and do the work. Do not be afraid or discouraged, for the LORD God, my God, is with you. He will not fail you or forsake you until all the work for the service of the temple of the LORD is finished." (1 Chronicles 28:20)*

Author's Afterword

(This is a piece I found after I wrote this book. It was written in March of 1995, two months after my conversion. I was twenty-three years old. Although some of it may be redundant, there are snippets in here that provide more detail and insight into how I developed SSA that you may find similar in your own life (or in the life of someone you love). I also want you to notice the knowledge I gained after just two months of following Jesus, and the difference in tone twenty-two years earlier.)

I really don't recall that much from the time before I was five years old. I was the youngest of three daughters, each seven years apart. Every time my mother was pregnant, my father hoped for a boy. I, being the last and a surprise to the family, probably felt his want for a boy more strongly. This also caused me to believe at one time that I was unloved and unwanted, thus deepening my low self-esteem. My father was in his late forties and my mother in her early forties when they were pregnant with me. My mother told her mother-in-law that she was pregnant for a third time and that she thought she was too old. My soon-to-be grandmother said, "No, you're not! It's nice to have another baby and a bigger family."

Shortly after birth, I had a physical trauma. I don't know too much about it except that I was about a month old, and I was in the hospital for almost a week. It was some kind of virus. The nurses took very good care of me, like they would their own child. My mother visited me daily, and she held me. She stayed over a few nights. My oldest sister, Lonnie, often went with her, and they prayed a lot. Even though my father was working full-time, I learned that he also often visited, sometimes with other members of his family. He drove them home in the evenings after work.

My father was bitter at this time because of the death of his sister, my namesake. Meanwhile, my mother put all her attention on me above anyone else because I was sick and the "baby" of the family. He was jealous at times and sought relief by going out drinking. We weren't too financially secure, and when I was about four years old, we moved into a house that my paternal grandmother paid for. I don't remember spending a lot of time with my father. It was more like I had three mothers (my mother and two older sisters). My earliest memory from the time we moved into this house is how the living room floor looked without a rug. Then, after the rug was put in, I remember rolling around on it, smelling and feeling it. I liked it.

Even though I don't recall any happy childhood memories with my father, I remember in first grade when I had to write for homework what I wanted to be when I grew up. I said that I wanted to be a mailman, "just like my father." Also, when I was in kindergarten I remember being sad when we sung "My County Tis of Thee," at the part that said, "land where my fathers died." I thought of my father and felt bad in some way that I might lose him or think of him as dying.

During this time I was doing "boyish" things, like playing with guns, cars, and toys from Santa Claus that reinforced "male" behavior. My family was unaware of this when they purchased racetracks and Incredible Hulk dolls for me. I wanted them. I also dressed on some family occasions in flannel shirts with a few of the buttons down to "act like a boy." I was never admonished for this; nevertheless, I was probably told I looked "cute." On other occasions, however, such as the more formal ones on my father's side of the family, my mother had to make sure every thread and every hair on my head was in place. They were always "proper"

Author's Afterword

in their dress, and we often felt ill at ease around them, overly conscious about ourselves.

Later on, a few short haircuts allowed me to be mistaken for a boy. I was unhappy about this. I felt embarrassed, like I wanted to hide and put my head under a rock. Although, I recall another time when I had just washed my hair and blow-dried it with wings (that was the style back in the late '70s and early '80s), and my second oldest sister, Marissa, took pictures of me because I looked so "tomatoey." (The word *tomato* was slang most popular in the 1940s for an attractive woman.) I felt it, too.

I had some good times playing with the neighborhood kids, although I remember a lot of fights. I can still hear what some were chanting one day: "Oooh, oooh, JM is so ugly." My oldest sister came to my rescue. I used to ride my bike around the block in fear some days that they would see me and attack me. Every time I passed my house, I would ring the bike bell three times to let my mother know if I was in trouble. I always looked to her for protection. I was always scared to handle it myself, and I never learned to stick up for myself. My memory holds no recollection of my father ever defending me. He just wasn't around.

I was overly attached to my mother at this time. During kindergarten, all I remember is crying, not wanting to go to school without her. We would stand outside the classroom, even the school sometimes, for what seemed like hours. Such stress. I can't recall one day where I left her happily to go to school. First grade was the same, but worse. I threw up practically every morning. Some days I hid in the closet or in the bathroom so I wouldn't have to go to school. One day I put my sister's vases, bowls, and knickknacks under the covers of my bed where I was supposed to be sleeping so everyone would think it was me. In the meantime, I was hiding in my closet. During the course of the school year, one day I stood on the street near the mailbox after lunch so I didn't have to go in. I wanted my mother all the time. I never wanted my father.

Throughout all my years of grammar school, I never felt socially accepted. I had crushes on boys but never fit in. My mother and I were always looking for a friend that I could "latch" on to. It seemed like everyone had their own little clique. My mother came to school at lunch time a lot. She was my best friend (I never had one until late high school), with whom I felt secure and at ease. When the kids saw her, they would shout, "JM, your mother! JM your mother!" I felt mortified and intimidated when they did this. I also got angry.

I was always the last one picked to be part of a gym group. This intensified my feelings of rejection. That is why today I like to socialize in even numbers for fear of being left out of something, even with my own family. I remember a time when a clique I thought I was a part of went out to lunch without me for some reason or other, and I rushed by bus all the way home to my mother and choked down a fast food sandwich because I didn't have a lot of time left after waiting for them. The class wanted me to get the name "Mute" on the back of my class of '85 jersey because I was always quiet.

On the home front, my main memories consist of my mother constantly complaining about my father. There was not one good or positive word that came out of her mouth about him. In fact, she swore at him on the nights he came home late because he had been drinking. When she was mad at him, she would rant about how his mother ruined her life when she sent him to live with his uncle in the city where he (eventually) met her. I'll never forget her exact words: "And she (her mother-in-law) ruined my life when she sent that little bum to New York! Dirty dog!" Sometimes I laughed at this; I even tape-recorded it. There wasn't one night that we were happy when he came home. It was always, "Oh no!" from me and my mother. My sisters felt the same way, even though they didn't say it. There was tension on the nights he came home drunk. He would start a fight over the stupidest things. He would swear at my mother and

Author's Afterword

sometimes throw things. I always remembered her complaining about the "verbal abuse," although she never took a stand or did something about it. Sometimes she suspected him of having a mistress. "He might be out seeing his skank!" I never suspected this, though. It didn't bother me. It was her own insecurity in her role as a wife. She just remained bitter, taking abuse again and again as it happened. She said she didn't want to frighten us kids and make matters worse. Meanwhile, her weak feminine portrayal thwarted my perception of my own femininity, and thus I was led to believe that it wasn't okay to be a woman. No way did I want to be like her!

I was always fearful that my father would "start up." When he did, I was very nervous and angry. There would be pains in my back from the repressed hostility. On pay night there would be extra tension. My mother just told us that he's good to us and loves us, so we shouldn't be mad or feel hatred towards him (denied, ignored, confused feelings). In the meantime, I was so angry at him for this, for upsetting my mother like that and causing turmoil in the family! But I never said a thing to him. He was always at a distance, a stranger. It was all internalized. He was always the master, she was always the servant.

There'd also be tension in the mornings, when he didn't drink. We call him "Skullino," a name given to him by my mother from the movie, *The Screaming Skull*. All of us, with one exception, call him that to this very day. Only my mother sometimes calls him that to his face, and he doesn't seem to mind. My sisters and I never called him anything to his face. Not even, "Dad," "Daddy," "Pop," or "Father." Nothing. Just "Skull" or "Skullino" when talking amongst each other (my oldest sister, Lonnie, calls him "Poppy" now because of her kids). I also have a very hard time looking at him in the eye when we speak. I just look at the table or something else. When I do look him in the eye, it is very brief.

All of this happened for as long as I could remember. As a result of all this, I grew up thinking all men were no good and that I couldn't trust any of them. To this day, it was always the "four of us"—my mother, two sisters, and me. I felt like we were a clique.

For most of my life, I only had fun times and good memories with women. Good times were with the females of the family, including my aunts and female cousins. "Women's Nights Out." So, I don't know how it is to feel comfortable with a man. I didn't like my brother-in-law when he was with my sister when I was nine to twelve years old. We were jealous of each other, each vying for my sister's attention. I remember when he went to kiss her in a park, I threw a basketball between them (meaning to break them up, but it accidentally hit her). I couldn't relate to him, either.

Another lasting memory that arises from this preteen stage is when I used to stay on the beach in the summer with my family (father included), bare-chested. I "had nothing there," my mother would say. At first I was uncomfortable to take my top off, but then it was okay because I had "nothing there." This happened a few times until I got uncomfortable again with it. I remember my cousin saying to my sister Marissa, "She doesn't see us doing it, so she figures she shouldn't do it either." It didn't happen again after that. I never really thought much of it because other young females on the beach did it too.

Lack of love and attention from my father and factors mentioned earlier led to the development of low self-esteem, the foundation for gender emptiness (GE). I hungered for suitable feminine security and modeled myself after the wrong parent—my father. It is between these two stages that an internal emotional wall went up between my sensitive, hurt, never-expressed-feelings of my inner child and my authoritative, critical inner parent that tells me I "should have" done this or that.

Author's Afterword

I was always an "A" student throughout grammar school, high school, and college. I was always an achiever, a perfectionist. I always felt worthwhile when I achieved because it was the only time I remember as a kid that I got praise and approval from my father. That is why even today, on a day that I do "nothing," I feel unimportant. I always wanted to please those in authority—my inner parent. I used perfectionism as a way to cover up or to protect the painful emotions of my inner child.

In junior high and early high school, since I experienced GE, I was uncomfortable with the same-sex peers because I did not feel adequate around them or equal to them or their activities and attitudes. When I participated with my peers, I received further rejection and unacceptance. This reinforced my GE feelings and "wounded area." It was at this stage (the first year of high school) that I was overly interested in girls. Here's when I had my first "crush." I looked to other females for identity, since mine was insecure. I formed an attraction and attachment to women in an intense way. One was Jill Stacchivo. I was obsessed with this girl. She was smart (she sat in front of me in every class the entire year), good-looking, and popular. She was part of the "in" clique. You could just imagine the immense feelings I had for her. Some of it is too embarrassing to write here (what her slightest touch did to me, biological urges that occurred when I wanted to call her). The quality of my day was based on my interactions with her and the others. My family and I didn't make much of it because we thought it was just a phase. I continually wanted their acceptance because it was something I never had.

My Sweet Sixteen, the first real party in a girl's life, turned out disastrous. Half of the people invited didn't show up, and the half that did left the party for a few hours to go out drinking. That really upset me. The nicest thing I do remember is dancing with a boy that I liked (or should I say "thought" I liked before I discovered sexual feelings for girls) since grammar school. His name was Dennis Skipper. Later when I had our picture in my locker, I found out he was seeing somebody in my class! Even up to this point in my life, I felt like an outcast with no sense of social belonging. Meanwhile, my attraction and crushes on females was really starting to grow. The prom was another disappointment.

By prom, this gender emptiness became sexual attraction, in which the attractive features I sought for myself became sexualized and eroticized. Because I never achieved gender emotional intimacy with my peers, I constantly found myself fantasizing about women.

I'll never forget the first person I "fell in love with." Her name was Christine Bellato, and she befriended me in our junior year of high school. She sat at our large, "clique-ish" lunch table. An excursion to Washington, D.C., was planned as our junior trip. I remember the girls yapping and chatting about it, talking about who was staying with whom in whose room. The few friends I had at the time were not really my friends. One didn't even include me in her plans! Again, I was in a social dilemma. My family (the girls) and I couldn't believe how I was being treated and how mean these girls were. Then one day, Christine came over to me and asked me to be in her room. I was ecstatic! I couldn't believe it. She also said that she was going to "kick" someone else out (the friend that didn't include me). She turned out to be someone I could trust. So, even though I didn't have the best time on this trip because of feelings of exclusion by the others, I became good friends with Christine.

A few years later when we became best friends (the first one I ever really had), I fell head over heels for her. Again, we thought it was just a normal phase because some adolescents develop crushes on their best friend. Meanwhile, I was forming a strong emotional dependency on her which was not healthy. I was jealous and always wanted verification of our friendship. I was especially jealous of her boyfriend, and I showed it when I hit her one time when she wanted to go over to his house. I thought we would be friends forever if we survived that. Three years ago, God took her away from me because of that strong bond I had towards her.

During this stage, I "fell in love" with several other peers/casual friends in high school. The same biological urges occurred again and again. It was always the same story. It was my excitement in hanging out with them, the looking forward to going to dances with them more so than usual, etc. Still, we all thought it was a normal phase, because I was still seeking dates with boys, even though I never felt the same towards any of them.

I formed another intense relationship with a woman in my junior year of college. Her name was Gail Mattruso. Here, I was finally part of the clique that I never had. We went out practically every Friday night in New York City. When we didn't do that, we went to a local hangout in Brooklyn. This was to me at the time the best times of my life, although it only lasted for eight months. The same feelings emerged for her, as did the others. I could never forget the feeling I got when dancing close to her in a hot crowded bar, all sweaty from dancing. (She was a great dancer and loved it like I did.) One night at a club in the city it was so hot and crowded and I think she was a little drunk, I managed to kiss her—only on the cheek. That was enough for me! She didn't even realize it. She was affectionate in her own friendly way through hand holding and arm tucking. I, on the other hand, was reveling in sexual rapturous feelings. She claimed to be my best friend, too, which heightened my esteem. This, another short-lived friendship, ended in emotional hurt and pain.

So, here I am at the last stage of my homosexual development, homosexual reinforcement. My identity and orientation is now being reinforced. I sought out people and places, searched for answers to the question, *Am I really gay?* I didn't go to my family (the girls) about this because I thought they were old fashioned and I thought that I knew it all. I trusted my feelings, and that was it. I didn't want to turn to them, and I didn't even think of turning to God. I was too involved with the world and secular beliefs.

I spoke to professors at college who were bisexual and gay, sent for gay yellow pages, wrote to gays across the country, went to "coming out" meetings in the city, read books, saw movies, etc. You name it, I did it. I couldn't take it anymore. My feelings were too strong; my hormones were on the rise. I wanted to meet people like myself.

After college is when I did most of my exploring (idle minds…)—for about one and a half years. I met a good gay friend that I went out with, and later on I met someone just as confused as I was. I also developed feelings for her, but I thank God now, she didn't have the same for me. I really thought I was born this way. I've been to gay counsellors and psychologists. Recently I even spoke to a nun and a priest who said it was okay! Now what am I supposed to think? The Bible is out of date, they said (and other remarks to that effect). I, with my strong tendencies, and after being brainwashed over the past two years that it is okay to be gay, found relief in what they were saying.

A little over three months ago, I even started a romantic relationship. I was dying to see what it felt like to kiss a woman. I've kissed a few men and felt nothing. The relationship was going great, despite the stress in having to lie to my family, thus creating distance between us. I just kept thinking that they have to accept it. It was so new, fun, and exciting. Sin is so pleasurable. After six weeks of seeing this older woman who was a mother figure to me (an extension of the overprotectiveness I received from my mother), a woman who seemed to have it all together (I lacked this in myself), who seemed to meet all my emotional and sexual needs, the Holy Spirit entered me. It was, and still is, hard because I was still in the fantastical beginning stages. I didn't feel the frustration and guilt that people feel after years in the lifestyle. It was hard for me to see. I thank God, though, that

Author's Afterword

I didn't have to go through that. I was also used to always getting what I want. Here the growth and maturity comes in. A stronger person will emerge. I now know how and why this relationship is not healthy, for my own psychological being and especially for my spiritual being. It was and is wrong.

At the present time, I am only a few months into my new relationship with Jesus Christ. I am now in the process of exploring His way. He is the way, the truth, and the life. His Holy Spirit is healing me little by little, very subtly. I trust in Him. I've learned so much and gained so much more than I ever would have if this didn't happen. I have His Word as my defense against Satan. It is a real struggle, but one cannot give up on God.

References

Arterburn, Jerry. *How Will I Tell My Mother.* Nashville, TN: Oliver Nelson, 1990.

Consiglio, William. *Homosexual No More.* Wheaton, IL: Victor Books, 1991.

Davies, Bob, and Lori Rentzel. *Coming Out of Homosexuality.* Downers Grove, IL: InterVarsity Press, 1993.

Homosexual Struggle. Downers Grove, IL: InterVarsity Press, 1978.

McMinn, Mark. *Dealing with Desires You Can't Control.* Colorado Springs, CO. NavPress, A Ministry of the Navigators, 1990.

Moberly, Elizabeth. *Homosexuality: A New Christian Ethic.* Cambridge, England: James Clarke & Co. Ltd, 1983.

Pausch, Randy. *The Last Lecture.* New York, NY: Hyperion Books, 2008.

Payne, Leanne. *The Broken Image.* Ada, MI: Baker Publishing Group, 1996.

Rentzel, Lori. *Emotional Dependency.* Downers Grove, IL: InterVarsity Press, 1990.

West, Christopher. *Created and Redeemed. The Universal Message of John Paul II's Theology of the Body.* (8 CD Set.) Milwaukie, WI: Ascension Press, 2005.

ORGANIZATION REFERENCES

Courage is an international apostolate of the Catholic Church, which ministers to persons with same-sex attractions. EnCourage is a Roman Catholic apostolate for parents, friends, and family members of loved ones with same-sex attractions.

Courage International, Inc.
8 Leonard Street
Norwalk, CT 06850
(203) 803-1564

https://couragerc.org
https://couragerc.org/encourage
http://encourageny.com

Email address: NYCourage@aol.com
Encourageny@hotmail.com
Communications@archny.org

Regeneration helps those seeking wholeness in the areas of intimacy, identity, and desire by inviting them into community marked by the truth and grace of Jesus.

Regeneration – Baltimore
P.O. Box 9830
Baltimore, MD 21284-9830
P: (410) 661-0284
F: 443-275-7918

http://regenerationministries.org
Email address: info@RegenerationMinistries.org

Regeneration – Northern Virginia
Phone: (703) 591-HOPE (4673)
Fax: 703-591-6540

http://regenerationministries.org
Email address: infoNoVA@RegenerationMinistries.org

Christian Ministry References

Answers in Genesis
P.O. Box 510
Hebron, KY 41048
Phone: (859) 727-2222
https://answersingenesis.org

Bible Science Association
http://bsa-ca.org

Dr. Charles Stanley
In Touch Ministries
P.O. Box 7900
Atlanta, GA 30357
Phone: (800) 789-1473
www.intouch.org

Dr. David Jeremiah
P.O. Box 3838
San Diego, CA 92163
Phone: (877) 998-0222
www.davidjeremiah.org
Email address: info@davidjeremiah.org

Dr. Mike Murdock
The Wisdom Center
4051 Denton Highway
Ft. Worth, TX 76117
Phone: (817) 759-0300
www.thewisdomcenter.tv
Email address: DrMurdock@TheWisdomCenter.tv

Family Radio
Family Stations Inc.
290 Hegenberger Rd.
Oakland, CA 94621
Phone: (800) 543-1495
www.familyradio.org

Institute for Creation Research
P.O. Box 59029
Dallas, Texas 75229
Phone: (800) 337-0375
www.icr.org

Joel Osteen Ministries
P.O. Box 4600
Houston, TX 77210
Phone: (888) 567-JOEL (5635)
www.joelosteen.com

Joyce Meyer Ministries
P.O. Box 655
Fenton, MO 63026
Phone: (800) 727-9673
www.joycemeyer.org

Other Organizations

Homosexuals Anonymous is an international organization dedicated to serving the recovery needs of men and women who struggle with unwanted same-sex attraction.

Homosexuals Anonymous
HAFS Downeast Maine
P.O. Box 176
Hancock, ME 04640
Phone: (207) 669-4264
www.homosexuals-anonymous.com
Email address: hafsdowneastmaine@gmail.com

Central Texas Chapter of HA Fellowship
Waco, TX
Phone: (254) 304-4770
https://haofcentraltexas.wordpress.com
Email address: paoiti254@yahoo.com

www.ingramcontent.com/pod-product-compliance
Lightning Source LLC
Chambersburg PA
CBHW072201100426
42738CB00011BA/2494